I0427798

TABLE OF CONTENTS

Page

TABLE OF CONTENTS...i

ACRONYMS...iii

ILLUSTRATIONS iv

TABLES v

CHAPTER 1 INTRODUCTION 1

    Background 2
    Research Questions..9
    Significance 10
    Assumptions..10
    Limitations 10
    Delimitations...11
    Key Terms...11

CHAPTER 2 LITERATURE REVIEW 14

    Introduction...14
    Hezbollah 15
    Israeli Lessons Learned 16
    U.S. COIN Doctrine..20
    Conclusion 22

CHAPTER 3 RESEARCH METHODOLOGY 23

    Introduction...23
    Methodology..23
    Key Events of 2006 War..24
    Evaluation Criteria..27
    Method of Evaluation 30

CHAPTER 4 ANALYSIS 32

    Introduction... 32
    Methodology 32
    War Game 33
        12 July 2006 33
            Hezbollah Initial Actions 33
            Israeli Response 35
            U.S. COIN Doctrinal Response 36
        14 July 2006 39
            Hezbollah Response 39
            Israeli Response 41
            U.S. COIN Directed Response 43
        17 July 2006 46
            Hezbollah Response 46
            Israeli Response 47
            U.S. COIN Directed Response 48
        21 July 2006 50
            Israeli Action..50
            Hezbollah Response 51
            U.S. COIN Directed Response 51
        30 July 2006 53
            Hezbollah Response 53
            Israeli Response 54
            U.S. COIN Directed Response 54
        4 August 2006 56
            Hezbollah Response 57
            Israeli Response 57
            U.S. COIN Directed Response 57
    Evaluation 60
    Examination of Evaluation/Conclusion 60

CHAPTER 5 CONCLUSION..64

    Introduction... 64
    Findings 65
    Recommendations... 67

BIBLIOGRAPHY...70

INITIAL DISTRIBUTION LIST 74

ACRONYMS

AMIA	Argentine Israelite Mutual Association
COIN	Counter Insurgency
EBO	Effects Based Operations
FM	Field Manual
IDF	Israeli Defense Force
IO	Information Operations
JP	Joint Publication
RAND	Research and Development Corporation
SLA	Southern Lebanon Army
TTP	Tactics, Techniques and Procedures
TWA	Trans World Airlines
UN	United Nations

ILLUSTRATIONS

Page

Figure 1. Nature of Hezbollah...4

TABLES

Page

Table 1. Evaluation Template 31

Table 2. Completed Evaluation..60

v

CHAPTER 1

INTRODUCTION

According to former Homeland Security Secretary Michael Chertoff, "Hezbollah is like the A-team of terrorists in terms of capabilities, in terms of range of weapons they have, in terms of internal discipline. To be honest, they make Al Qaeda look like a minor league team. They have been more disciplined, and they've been in some senses more restrained in the kinds of attacks they carry out in recent years, but that's not something we can take for granted," he warned (Ninan 2008). Hezbollah symbolizes the future of insurgency operations. This future is characterized by a threat that is state supported, combines guerilla style operations with conventional weapons and capabilities (becoming known as "hybrid" war), and matches any Army in ability to conduct HUMINT, information operations and computer network operations. Chief of Staff of the Army General Casey recognized this as a change in the character of conflict caused by the commitment of nonstate actors. Specifically, in a 2009 issue of Joint Forces Quarterly, GEN Casey stated that in the 2006 Lebanon conflict "you have a nonstate actor, Hezbollah, operating inside a state, Lebanon, fighting another state, Israel, and supported by yet another state, Iran. and Hezbollah starts the war with 13,000 rockets: The tools of power are no longer exclusively in the hands of states, and nonstate actors are a bit harder to deter than state actors" (Gurney 2009, 19). As understood by GEN Casey, the character of war is changing and through repeated wars with Israel, Hezbollah has provided us a specter of future war at what is assessed to be its most dangerous. Israeli experience against Hezbollah should trigger a review of counterinsurgency (COIN) doctrine and possible doctrinal reform much as the Arab-Israeli War of 1973 did for armor doctrine.

Background

Since being founded by Iran in 1982, Hezbollah killed more Americans than any other terrorist group until Al Qaeda's attack on the World Trade Center in 2001 (Weitz 2006). To this day, Hezbollah remains funded by Iran with Syrian assistance and a large network of state and non-state supporters and suppliers. It is largely regarded as Iran's proxy and vanguard military wing and shares Iran's radical Islamist ideology. This ideology views the US as their primary enemy, enabling the existence of Israel. The Iranian Revolutionary Guard Quds Force taught Hezbollah how to organize itself like an army, with special units for intelligence, antitank warfare, explosives, engineering, communications and rocket launching. Hezbollah's fighters number from 2,000 to 4,000 aided by a larger circle of part-timers who provide logistics and storage of weapons in houses and civilian buildings. These part-timers are a big part of what makes Hezbollah such a formidable threat in urban warfare. On order, some fighters emerge to retrieve launchers, fire missiles and then melt away back among the population, making targeting a challenge (Erlanger 2006, 1-6).

A large part of the concern regarding Hezbollah is based on the fact that they have, to a large part, achieved the goal of all insurgent groups; the overthrow of a constituted government through the use of subversion and armed conflict (Defense Department 2001, 6-22). Hezbollah has been entrusted by Iran to topple the Lebanese Free State and erect in its place an Iranian satellite state, in order to complete the sought after Shiite Crescent. Hezbollah currently controls 40 percent of the Lebanese territories and has in effect established a state within a state. Hezbollah, alongside Amal, is one of two major political parties in Lebanon that represent the Shiite Muslims. It holds 14 of the 128 seats in Lebanon's Parliament and is a member of the Resistance and Development Bloc. According to Daniel L. Byman, it is growing into "the most powerful single political movement in Lebanon" (Byman 2008).

In the general election of 2005, Hezbollah won 10.9 percent of parliamentary seats. The Resistance and Development Bloc, of which Hezbollah is a member, won all 23 seats in Southern Lebanon, and in total, 35 seats or 27.3 percent of parliamentary seats nationwide. When municipal elections were held in the first half of 2004, Hezbollah won control of 21 percent of the municipalities (Cobban 2005). Despite the attempt at political legitimacy, Hezbollah remains an armed militant organization. In August 2008, Lebanon's new Cabinet unanimously approved a draft policy statement which secures Hezbollah's existence as an armed organization and guarantees its right to "liberate or recover occupied lands" (Staff CFR 2008).

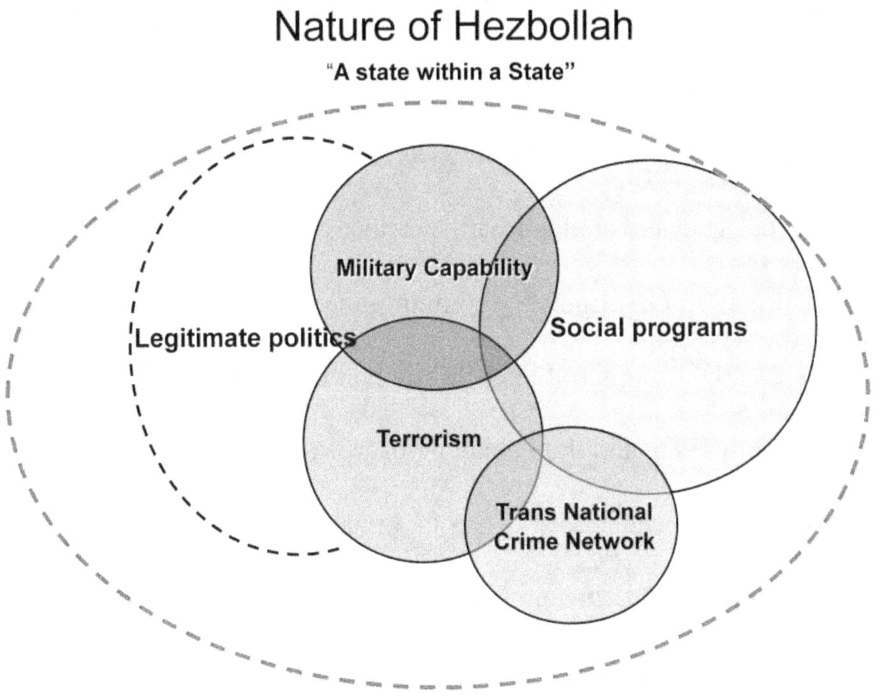

Nature of Hezbollah

"A state within a State"

Figure 1.   Nature of Hezbollah
Source: Division, IDF 91st. *Galilee Division Briefing,* Unit Presentation, Israeli IDF, 2009.

Through their political advancement, Hezbollah has maintained the objectives of their 1985 manifesto. This manifesto, issued on February 16, 1985 by Sheik Ibrahim al-Amin, laid out three objectives of the organization:

• To expel Americans, the French and their allies (sic) definitely from Lebanon, putting an end to any colonialist entity on out land.

• To submit the phalanges to a just power and bring them all to justice for the crimes they have perpetrated against Muslims and Christians.

• To permit all the sons of our people to determine their future and to choose in all the liberty the form of government they desire. We call upon all of them to pick the option of Islamic government which alone is capable of guaranteeing justice and liberty for all. Only an Islamic regime can stop any future tentative attempts of imperialistic infiltration onto our country.

The 1985 manifesto makes it clear that Hezbollah intends to use armed forces to achieve these goals (Jorisch 2003).

Hezbollah's military branch is known as Al-Muqawama al-Islamiyya, or "The Islamic Resistance." They are credited with attacks as recently as January 2008, including: the April 1983 U.S. Embassy bombing, the 1983 Beirut barracks bombing, and a spate of attacks on IDF troops and SLA militiamen in southern Lebanon, the hijacking of TWA Flight 847 in 1985, and the Lebanon hostage crisis from 1982 to 1992. Most recently, Hezbollah has been accused of the 15 January 2008 bombing of a U.S. Embassy vehicle in Beirut. Outside of Lebanon, Hezbollah has been accused of the 1992 Israeli Embassy attack in Buenos Aires, and the 1994 AMIA bombing of a Jewish cultural center, both in Argentina (Staff CFR 2008). These attacks, and the continued pledge of violence by senior Hezbollah leaders, demonstrate that despite engaging in continued political activity, Hezbollah remains an insurgent group willing to use violence to reach its goals.

By all accounts, Hezbollah has the military strength to do so. It has been estimated that Hezbollah's military force is made up of about 2,000 paid full-time members, along with an additional 6,000 – 10,000 consistent volunteers (Rao 2006). Hezbollah possesses a significant amount of Katyusha-122 rockets, which has a range of 29 km and carries a 15-kg (33-Ib) warhead. They also possess about 100 long-range missiles which include the Iranian-made Fajr-3 and Fajr-5, the latter with a range of 75 km, enabling it to strike the Israeli port of Haifa, and the Zelzal-1, with an estimated 150 km range, which can reach Tel Aviv. Fajr-3 missiles have a range of 40 km and a 45-kg

(99-Ib) warhead, and Fajr-5 missiles, which extend to 72 km, also hold 45-kg (99-Ib) warheads (Staff CFR 2008). According to various reports, Hezbollah is armed with anti-tank guided missiles, namely, the Russian-made AT-3 Sagger, AT-4 Spigot, AT-5 Spandrel, AT-13 Saxhorn-2 "Metis-M," AT-14 Spriggan "Kornet"; Iranian made Ra'ad (version of AT-3 Sagger), Towsan (version of AT-5 Spandrel), Toophan (version of BGM-71 TOW); and European-made MILAN missiles. These weapons have been used against IDF soldiers, causing many of the deaths during the 2006 Lebanon War (Weitz 2006). Iran's IRCG-Quds Force continues to train Hezbollah on the application and use of these systems, making them one of the most highly trained forces in the world.

Hezbollah has mastered its conventional and non-conventional forms of military operations, known as Hybrid Warfare, through consistent and prolonged conflicts with Israel. The first conflict began around the same time Iran established Hezbollah and occurred from 1982-2000, commonly referred to as the South Lebanon Conflict. Hezbollah had no established conventional force so they waged a guerrilla campaign against Israeli forces that were occupying Southern Lebanon. The conflict ended when Israel withdrew in 2000 under pressure to adhere to the 1978 United Nations Security Resolution 425, calling for Israeli withdrawal and a UN Peace Force to move in (Staff CFR 2008).

The next major conflict occurred on July 25, 1993 following Hezbollah's killing of seven Israeli soldiers in Southern Lebanon. In response to Hezbollah's actions, Israel launched Operation Accountability (known in Lebanon as the Seven Day War) during which it conducted its heaviest air and indirect fire attacks since the early days of the conflict in 1983. Israel's objective was to destroy Hezbollah in Southern Lebanon and force the population to demand the Government of Lebanon get Hezbollah under control. The battle lasted seven days and ended when each side essentially agreed to stop attacking civilians (Staff CFR 2008).

The peace did not last and Hezbollah began to develop a great conventional military capability. They began to fire rockets into northern Israel and in April 1996, Israeli armed forces launched Operation Grapes of Wrath, which was intended to wipe out Hezbollah's base in southern Lebanon. A cease-fire was agreed upon between Israel and Hezbollah, which would be effective on April 27, 1996. Once again, both sides agreed that civilians should not be targeted, which Hezbollah recognized as tacit acknowledgement of its right to continue its military activities against IDF forces inside Lebanon (Staff CFR 2008).

By the 2006 Lebanon War, Hezbollah had developed a strong paramilitary force. Hezbollah became rather emboldened and conducted a cross border raid during which they kidnapped and killed Israeli soldiers. In a speech in July 2008, Hezbollah leader Hassan Nasrallah acknowledged that he had ordered the kidnapping of Israeli soldiers in order to free Hezbollah prisoners held in Israeli jails. During this 36 day conflict Hezbollah fired thousands of Katyusha rockets against military and civilian targets. Hezbollah initiated this conflict by firing rockets at Israeli border towns as a diversion for an anti-tank missile attack on Israeli Humvees patrolling the border (Myre 2006). This demonstrated Hezbollah's increased weapons capability, training and confidence.

In addition to this robust military capability, Hezbollah has mastered the use of media to advance its position. Hezbollah operates a satellite television station, Al-Manar TV ("the Lighthouse") and a radio station, al-Nour (the "light"). These stations were started in 1991 with funding from Iran. Al-Manar, self pro-claimed "Station of the Resistance," is a key player in what Hezbollah calls its "psychological warfare against the Zionist enemy" and an integral part of Hezbollah's plan to spread its message to the entire Arab world (Jorisch 2003). This programming aired on Al-Manar is designed to inspire suicide attacks in Gaza, the West Bank, and Iraq (Jorisch 2003).

Hezbollah publishes and distributes material aimed at instilling principles of nationalism and Islam in children. The Hezbollah Central Internet Bureau released a video game in early 2003 entitled "Special Force," in which players conduct was on Israeli invaders, wherein the winner becomes a national hero on earth and martyr in heaven (Jorisch 2003). This mastery of influence through religion, media and technology is a key component of what has made Hezbollah such a formidable opponent for Israel and a threat to the U.S.

Funding is another area in which Hezbollah demonstrates its reach and robust network. Hezbollah has and continues to receive tens of millions of dollars annually from Iran in addition to weapons and training. The U.S. estimates that Iran has been giving Hezbollah about US$60-100 million per year in direct financial assistance (Mandari 2002). In addition, Hezbollah relies on Lebanese born people in West Africa, the U.S. and, most importantly, the so-called Triple Frontier, or tri-border area, along the junction of Paraguay, Argentina, and Brazil. Due to lack of law enforcement and border controls, the area is a haven for drug and arms trafficking, smuggling, counterfeiting and other illegal activities. The Arab population of the zone is believed to number over 20,000 (about one in every 30 residents), most of whom are Lebanese Muslims. Hezbollah's involvement in the area first came to the attention of US intelligence when Argentine authorities concluded that the bombings of the Israeli Embassy in 1992 and the Argentine-Israeli Community Center in Buenos Aires in 1994 were carried out by Hezbollah cells headquartered in the tri-border area. The area is now watched closely but it is clear that this region of the world is a haven for criminal activities linked to Hezbollah and other Islamist groups (State Department 2001).

The network that provides funding also helps to demonstrate Hezbollah's global reach. In addition to state sponsorship from Iran and Syria, Hezbollah's funding network demonstrates the extensive influence they hold in the U.S., Africa, the Middle East and South America. The fact that Hezbollah has been able to carry out attacks on Israeli Embassies as far west as Argentina demonstrates their global reach and highlights why this insurgent group needs to be of such high concern to the U.S.

Research Questions

Is US Counter Insurgency (COIN) Doctrine adequate to defeat Hezbollah as a threat model of future Insurgencies? In order to adequately answer this question, we must examine Hezbollah's strengths, and capabilities as well as their weaknesses and vulnerabilities and analyze whether current US COIN doctrine adequately addresses these areas to including exploiting weaknesses and vulnerabilities?

Significance

Non-state actors and insurgent organizations are expected to be a key player in all future conflicts. Hezbollah has emerged as the most capable of these organizations in that they have effective combined guerilla tactics with conventional weapons and capabilities as well as information operations and intelligence. Further, they are a non-state actor that has aggressively initiated operations against states to include Israel and the US in Iraq in an attempt to force Israel out of existence. As a result of Hezbollah's success, other insurgent organizations are likely to adopt Hezbollah's tactics, techniques and procedures and try to replicate their success. The U.S. must be prepared to deal with this threat in any future operation it conducts. A thorough study of Hezbollah should be conducted as a means of raising issues regarding the U.S. Army's COIN capabilities.

Assumptions

For the purposes of this study, and its relevance to future military operations, we must assume that insurgency and hybrid warfare will play a major role in future US conflicts. This is a reasonable assumption considering the expansion and rise of radical extremists and their increasing unhappiness with U.S. presence in the Middle East. We must also assume that the U.S. will maintain a presence in the Middle East and continue to fight the war on terror for years to come.

Limitations

This study will analyze Hezbollah as an insurgent threat, specifically focusing on hybrid warfare. It will use the 2006 Lebanon War between Israel and Hezbollah as a case study. This study will examine COIN doctrine in the context of Hezbollah and its success in conducting hybrid warfare using evaluation criteria to determine its adequacy.

Delimitations

Due to time and length restraints, this paper will not conduct a comparison with other terrorist organizations but will persuade the audience that Hezbollah is the most formidable insurgent threat by way of detailed layout of Hezbollah capabilities and achievements. Also, the lessons learned by Israel will essentially be taken on face value, due to lack of other sources of knowledge to refute them. In addition, this study will examine the military aspects of COIN doctrine in the limits of the evaluation criteria as detailed in Chapter 3 and is not meant to be a complete analysis of U.S. COIN doctrine or the whole of government approach to operations. In addition, due to classification restrictions, this paper will not be able to examine the significant role Hezbollah, in conjunction with Iran, is playing in over throwing the current constituted government in Iraq.

Key Terms

Insurgency: An organized movement consisting of interlocking system of actions--political, economic, psychological, and military--that aims at the overthrow of the constituted government in a country and its replacement by another regime.

Note: This definition combines Roger Trinquier (as one of the most respected theorists of counter-insurgency) definition: "interlocking system of actions--political, economic, psychological, military--that aims at the overthrow of the established authority in a country and its replacement by another regime" (Trinquer 1961, 12), and the Department of Defense definition from JP 1-02: "an organized movement aimed at the overthrow of a constituted government through the use of subversion and armed conflict", to create what I believe is a more complete and specific definition.

Counter Insurgency: from JP 1-02: Those military, paramilitary, political, economic, psychological, and civic actions taken by a government to defeat insurgency.

Explosively Formed Penetrators: squat canisters designed to explode and spit out molten balls of copper that cut through armor.

Full Spectrum Operations: The conduct of simultaneous combinations of the four components of Army operations (offense, defense, stability, and civil support) across the spectrum of conflict (peace, crisis, and war).

Human Intelligence: JP 1-02: A category of intelligence derived from information collected and provided by human sources.

Hybrid Warfare: For the purposes of this study, Hybrid War(fare) will be defined as the simultaneous employment of traditional, irregular, catastrophic, and disruptive tactics, techniques, and procedures in an effort to achieve success across the full range of warfare: tactical; operational; and strategic.

Information Operations: The employment of the core capabilities of electronic warfare, computer network operations, psychological operations, military deception, and operations security, in concert with specified supporting and related capabilities, to affect and defend information and information systems and to influence decision-making.

Khomeini Religious Ideology: a belief in revolt, and especially martyrdom, against injustice and tyranny as part of Shia Islam. Further, it is a belief that clerics should mobilize and lead their flocks into action, not just advise them. Ideology rejects the influence of both Soviet and American superpowers in Iran with the slogan "not Eastern, nor Western--Islamic Republican."

Revolutionary Guard Corps Quds Force (IRGC-Quds): responsible for extraterritorial operations for Iran, including terrorist operations. A primary focus for the Quds Force is training Islamic fundamentalist terrorist groups. Currently, the Quds Force conducts training activities in Iran and in Sudan. The Quds Force is also responsible for gathering information required for targeting and attack planning. Chapter two will examine literature available in regards to all major components of this study.

CHAPTER 2

LITERATURE REVIEW

This is a game of wits and will. You've got to be learning and adapting to survive. (FM 3-24)

— General Peter J. Schoomaker

Introduction

This paper will answer the primary question of whether US COIN doctrine is adequate to defeat Hezbollah as a threat model of future insurgencies. Key components of this are Hezbollah and their capabilities, lessons learned by Israel as Hezbollah's most frequent opponent, and U.S. COIN doctrine itself. The subject of Hezbollah is one widely studied and published from multiple perspectives. A thorough understanding of Hezbollah can be achieved by reading books from various perspectives on Hezbollah, all readily available. In addition, the subject of Hezbollah military capabilities as faced by Israel has been widely published in journals and periodicals. The study of Israeli lessons learned as well as interviews and after action reviews are abundant and provide a firsthand perspective on Hezbollah in action. Following the December 2006 publication of FM 3-24, multiple military scholars have stepped forward to analyze the strengths and weaknesses of U.S. COIN doctrine. These studies are very useful in identifying the areas that COIN doctrine may fall short in addressing Hezbollah as a threat. There appears to be no research done that directly compares Hezbollah, Israeli lessons learned and U.S. COIN doctrine.

<u>Hezbollah</u>

There are three primary categories of relevant books available on Hezbollah itself. These include: those written by Hezbollah insiders or pro-Hezbollah authors; those written by Lebanese people or people in Lebanon with direct access to information and opinions; and those written by Hezbollah opponents such as Israelis.

When seeking insight to Hezbollah and their ideology, Naim Qassem, a founding member of Hezbollah in 1982 and the current Deputy Secretary General, is perhaps the most insightful of all authors. In his work, *"Hezbollah, the Story from Within,"* Qassem provides insight as to Hezbollah's vision and goals, beliefs, and perhaps most importantly, he is able to describe the various compartments and aspects to both the political and terrorist wings of Hezbollah to include future plans and goals. In his work, Qassem has provided an insight to the thoughts and perspectives of Hezbollah. Any study of Hezbollah must include an understanding of these thoughts and ideologies that drive its members (Qassem 2005, 12-42).

In the second category, Lebanese based authors with a less biased insight, Judith Palmer Harik, a twenty year professor at American University in Beirut and known worldwide as an expert on Hezbollah is a great source. As an American who married a Christian Lebanese, Harik does not have any pre-determined bias toward Hezbollah. As a result, her access provides insight that is not biased by her ideology. Her book, *"Hezbollah, The Changing Face of Terrorism,"* offers a factual look at Hezbollah's mechanics, politics, and military operations (Harik 2005, 23-65).

Finally, to ensure a complete perspective on Hezbollah as an organization, work by Israeli authors who can provide an opponent's view of Hezbollah is necessary. Michel

Warschawski is an Israeli anti-Zionist activist who worked with displaced Lebanese

National, Gilbert Achcar, on *The 33 Day War*". In his book, Warschawski provides an

Israeli perspective on the formation of Hezbollah and how they have risen in Lebanon.

His access to Israeli military personnel provides an insightful look at how Hezbollah

conducted operations in the thirty three day war with Israeli and what makes them such a

formidable opponent (Achcar 2007, 33-78).

<u>Israeli Lessons Learned</u>

Several journal articles and periodicals are available in reference to Israeli lessons

learned during wars with Hezbollah. A number of these works serve as primary sources

in that they are interviews, commission reports and manuscripts of proceedings. These

works can be divided into two categories: those written by Israeli authors to include

military personnel and interviews (primary sources), and those written by U.S.

institutions as an effort to learn from these conflicts. All of these works provide valuable

information for the purpose of this thesis.

First looking at Israeli self assessments, there is a strong disagreement between

military leaders and other Israeli government officials in terms of IDF performance and

what their failures can be attributed to. As can be expected, the most specific and

dedicated assessments were conducted by the Israeli military itself but these assessments

often remove blame from the IDF and military leaders.

Two military reviews of lessons learned by IDF elements involved in the 2006

War provided background information. The first was the transcript of a conference held

in November 2006 by the Armor Corps Association in Israel at which the theme was

"Winning Land Warfare after the Second Lebanon War." Senior members of the Israeli

Armor Corps provided their opinion in regards to what is commonly considered by Israeli military elements as the three main issues identified as a result of the 2006 Lebanon War: the state of IDF doctrine, the changed nature of Israel's security environment, and the adaption by Hezbollah to Israeli and IDF practices. The report of these proceedings provides one of the better critiques of Israeli doctrine found during research. The proceeding concluded that IDF COIN doctrine was inadequate in addressing a hybrid threat such as Hezbollah and that their doctrine had become too complex and lacked clarity (Glenn 2008, 11-48).

The 91st "Galillee" Division presented a briefing to superiors in February 2007 that also highlighted multiple doctrinal failures in regards to conducting counterinsurgency operations. The 91st Division focused its presentation on how effects based operations have hindered ground maneuver operations. The conclusion of this Division, shared by several Israeli military experts to include Brigadier General Shimon Naveh, Commander of IDF forward forces in 2006 War, is that the use of air power was an attempt to bypass tactical operations and destroy Hezbollah at the strategic level. Lt. Gen. (Res) Amon Lipkin also emphasized that failure to properly employ ground forces early and with adequate tasks and directives attributed to IDF failures (Division IDF 91st 2009).

In addition, military reviews of lessons learned from the conflict tend to focus on intelligence failures. The lack of intelligence included significant underestimates as to the number and location of Hezbollah weapons caches, their possession of advanced technology and their sophisticated use of tunnels and bunkers. Lt. Gen. Lipkin goes on to discuss that failure to synchronize intelligence between Israel's three intelligence agencies, distribution of intelligence to commanders, and poor knowledge management aided IDF failures. Intelligence failure and over dependence on air are the two areas emphasized by all civilian and military reviews of the 2006 war (Division IDF 91st 2009).

Israeli civilian organizations and analysts tend to focus on issues that can be more directly blamed on the IDF and its leadership. The Jaffee Center for Strategic Studies at the University in Tel Aviv emphasizes the misallocation of military resources and the IDF's failure to adapt techniques to the specific threat possessed by Hezbollah as opposed to the Palestinians (commonly referred to as "fighting the last war") (Ophir 2006).

A significant number of U.S. institutions have also conducted studies on Israeli-Hezbollah wars and analyzed these wars as a means of driving U.S. policy and actions. The majority of these publications focus on strategic level issues with tactical implications as opposed to Israeli reviews that focus on operational level issues with tactical and strategic implications. Of note are publications by The Brookings Institute, The Center for Strategic and International Studies, and the United States Army.

The Brookings Institution is notable for their published panel discussions of experts on Israel-Hezbollah Wars and several publications of Israeli scholars both via the Brookings Saban Center for Middle East Policy. In September 2006, a panel discussion was held in which four Israeli scholars, too include two previous U.S. Ambassadors to Israel, conducted a discussion on the aftermath of the 2006 Israeli-Hezbollah conflicts and the residual effects on Hezbollah's capabilities and resulting U.S. Policy. The transcript of this panel discussion provides four primary sources and their detailed accounts of where Hezbollah was able to be successful against the IDF and what measures are required to ensure that Hezbollah is defeated in the future. This panel focused on strategic level issues, emphasizing problems within the Lebanese Government (Court 2006, 1-43).

A second Brookings Institution publication worth noting is "*Lebanese Identity and Israeli Security in the Shadows of the 2006 War*" by Shibley Telhami. Telhami is an Israeli and specialist in the politics of the Middle East, especially the Israeli-Arab conflict. Born into an Arab family in Israel, he has a unique insight to the ideology and religious implications of this conflict. This publication highlights a survey he conducted in Lebanon. His survey demonstrates the depth of division within Lebanon; a division he feels is perpetuated by Hezbollah. He goes on to show how Hezbollah has been successful in capitalizing on this division and the political instability it has created (Telhami 2006, 21-26).

Anthony Cordesman of the Center for Strategic and International Studies has conducted a thorough study of lessons learned from the Hezbollah-Israeli war. In "Preliminary Lessons of the Israeli-Hezbollah War," Cordesman identifies several critical areas that have led to Israeli inability to defeat Hezbollah. In his paper, Cordesman examines how limitations placed on a state (Israel) when opposing a non-state threat (Hezbollah) place limits on the state that have prevented Israel from defeating Hezbollah. He specially examines proportionality, collateral damage, media and limits placed on states or rational actors in war. This paper provides one of the more thorough and combat focused assessments published (Cordesman 2006, 1-38).

The United States Army, through the Combat Studies Institute at Fort Leavenworth and the Strategic Studies Institute at the War College, have published numerous studies focused on capturing the military lessons learned by Israel as a means of improving U.S. Policy and military capability. In Occasional Paper 26 of the Long War Series, *"We Were Caught Unprepared: The 2006 Hezbollah-Israeli War"* the Combined Arms Center at Fort Leavenworth examines intricate tactical and strategic details that affected Israel's preparation and execution of the 2006 war with Lebanon. In this paper, it is concluded that Israel's doctrine was focused on defeating the Palestinians, a more conventional insurgent threat, and was inadequate for defeating a Hezbollah, who employs "hybrid" capabilities. This is one of the few similarities between Israeli issues raised in literature, and issues raised by U.S. authors and organizations conducting reviews (Matthews 2008, 18-23). On the same note, in "The 2006 Lebanon Campaign and the Future of Warfare: Implications for Army and Defense Policy," The Strategic Studies Institute focuses on Hezbollah's "Hybrid" capability. This study highlights how Hezbollah did not perform exceptionally well at the traditional insurgent tactics of guerilla warfare, nor did it form exceptionally well at conventional operations. Rather Hezbollah's success against Israel was based on its ability to apply both methods of warfare simultaneously against an enemy whose doctrine left them unprepared for a hybrid threat (Biddle 2008).

<u>U.S. COIN Doctrine</u>

Following the December 2006 publication of FM 3-24, multiple institutions and military experts came forward to offer critiques of the new U.S. Army COIN Doctrine. Most notably of these is a series of publications by the RAND Corporation as the result of a research study conducted for the U.S. Department of Defense on how to improve counterinsurgency operations. The study had yielded five papers addressing various aspects of COIN, many of which can be directly applied to defeating Hezbollah. I will highlight two of those at this time.

Volume I of the counterinsurgency study addresses regaining information superiority against an insurgent threat. One of Hezbollah's significant successes against Israel can be traced back to its incredible use of information operations, making this study very relevant to the issue at hand.

The final report of the RAND Counterinsurgency study recognizes four types or categories of insurgencies. By categorizing insurgencies, the RAND Corporation believes that doctrine can be more specific and focused rather than general as COIN doctrine, as currently written, can be. By the standards outlined in this report, Hezbollah is a type III threat. The paper goes on to provide several areas that must be addressed to defeat this type of threat that will be addressed in the remainder of this paper (Gomport 2008).

In addition to the Counterinsurgency study, the RAND Corporation has published several other applicable papers. In "Understanding Proto-insurgencies," the RAND Corporation identifies several indicators for analysts monitoring potential insurgent groups (Byman 2008). They highlight Hezbollah by looking at what made them so successful and what indicators should be looked for in the future. By directing attention to identifying what made Hezbollah such a successful threat, the information reported by RAND can directly assist in the development of effective COIN doctrine.

Conclusion

There is a significant amount of information published on all three areas that encompass this study: Hezbollah, Israeli lessons learned against Hezbollah, and U.S. COIN doctrine. The subject of Hezbollah is well covered by authors from Lebanese, Israeli and U.S. descent ensuring a broad, all encompassing assessment of the group and its operations. In addition, lessons learned by Israeli during their multiple conflicts with Hezbollah are well published. Israeli publications include transcripts from conferences and panels involving military and civilian leaders with multiple perspectives on the issue. Published information includes analysis of tactical, strategic and operational level lessons learned by military leaders and civilians critical of IDF operations. Coupled with extensive analysis by U.S. organizations, a broad perspective of lessons learned from all echelons in command area available and considered for this paper. The subject of U.S. COIN doctrine has been examined by numerous scholars and experts and includes a RAND study of COIN doctrine. It appears however, that no one has published any work focused on incorporating these three subjects into an extensive study of COIN doctrine in regards to Hezbollah. The following chapter will outline the method this paper will use to analyze these subjects.

CHAPTER 3

RESEARCH METHODOLOGY

[T]here is no universal approach to counterinsurgency. All wars flow from the economic, political and social conditions of the adversaries. Due to its character as an essentially political struggle for power, COIN is even more dependent on these conditions than conventional war. Thus, what works against one insurgency will not necessarily work against another.

— T. X. Hammes
Colonel, U.S. Marines (Retired)

Introduction

This paper will answer the primary question of whether US COIN doctrine is adequate to defeat Hezbollah as a threat model of future insurgencies. Key components of this are Hezbollah and their capabilities, lessons learned by Israel as Hezbollah's most frequent opponent, and U.S. COIN doctrine itself. In the 2006 Lebanon War, Israel was defeated by Hezbollah in most of the world's eyes. Considering Israel's history and frequent fights with insurgent groups trying to over through them and their existence, it came as a shock that Hezbollah was so successful against them. As a result, studying the failures of their doctrine as it applies to Hezbollah provides a strong foundation for reviewing our own doctrine and can serve as a basis for evaluating whether U.S. doctrine is adequate.

Methodology

To evaluate the effectiveness of U.S. COIN doctrine against Hezbollah, this paper will examine six key events from the 2006 Lebanon War (Fickling 2006). Events selected best demonstrate Hezbollah's unique capabilities indicated by underlined text. Using these six events, this paper will conduct a war game in which six evaluation criteria will be used to determine if U.S. COIN doctrine, as currently written, is adequate to defeat Hezbollah as a model of insurgent threat. The evaluation criteria were selected based on widely accepted ingredients critical to successful counterinsurgency operations and U.S. lessons learned in Iraq. To help judge whether U.S. response per COIN doctrine is adequate, this paper will examine Israel's response to Hezbollah and their lessons learned from the conflict. If Israeli response was effective, this paper will examine if our response is similar enough or what it is lacking to have the same effect. If Israel's effect was inadequate, this paper will examine, using their lessons learned, what the short-coming were and assess whether U.S. COIN doctrine varies enough to be effective. U.S. COIN doctrine will be given an "E" to indicate that doctrine, as outlined, will be effective against Hezbollah as a threat model; an "A" for adequate-- meaning the response would have a positive effect though not a complete one; and an "I" for inadequate-- meaning that doctrine needs to be changed in order to effectively or even adequately address the threat.

Key Events of 2006 War

The six key events that will be used in the war game and capability they are intended to demonstrate are:

1. 12 July 2006--Hezbollah launches rockets across the Lebanese border, targeting several Israeli border towns, and then stages an attack in which three Israeli soldiers are killed and two more kidnapped.

This attack demonstrates the years of training and dedicated study of Israeli operations by Hezbollah. Choosing to conduct the kidnapping in the July months was a very strategic decision in that the mid-summer months greatly favor the static defender over a

24

dismounted aggressor. Hezbollah obviously spent a considerable amount of time thinking

about when to attack, how the IDF would fight, what weapons the IDF would use, as well

as what personnel, fortifications and tactics they would need to apply. Hezbollah mined

the road networks leading into southern Lebanon forcing Israel to enter through the

country-side and not use roads. They constructed massive fighting positions capable of

sustaining fighters for weeks at a time. These positions had eighteen inches of concrete

for overhead cover to provide protection from Israeli air strikes mitigating Israel's main

weapon. This also demonstrates Hezbollah's hybrid capability in that they utilize

conventional weapon systems of a conventional army while employing guerrilla warfare

operations.

2. 14 July 2006--Hezbollah fires rockets, causing major damage in the Israeli city of
    Haifa. Israel Prime Minister Ehud Olmert announces that in order for Israel to call
    a ceasefire, Hezbollah must disarm, end its rocket attacks on Israeli civilians, and
    return the kidnapped soldiers. Meanwhile, Syria pledges its full support of
    Hezbollah and Iranian President Mahmoud Ahmadinejad warns Israel not to
    attack Syria.

July 14th marked a day the world began to understand the complex network of world

supporters Hezbollah has. Weapons utilized were bought from Russia by Syria with

Iranian money and provided to Hezbollah. The amount of rockets and munitions clearly

demonstrate a large amount of state support as well as a broad funding network. The

manner in which Hezbollah utilized weapon systems indicates extensive training by

Iranian conventional forces.

3. 17 July 2006--Israeli elite Special Forces known as the Maglan Unit, conducts
    limited battalion size ground operations into Hezbollah territory in Lebanon to
    find a network of tunnels and were quickly surrounded by Hezbollah fighters. The
    IDF was forced to commit three plus additional brigades to relieve the Maglan

force as Hezbollah utilized antitank missiles to penetrate Israeli armor and defeat committed forces.

Ability to surround Israel's most elite ground force demonstrates Hezbollah's tremendous tactical proficiency. Hezbollah utilized small arms, mortars, rockets, and antitank weapons in combined arms operations rather than the standard hit and run tactics commonly utilized by insurgent organizations. This demonstrates that Hezbollah operates in cells that are task organized by mission and able to conduct simultaneous operations.

4. 21 July 2006--Israeli army calls up its reservists, preparing for possible ground offensive in Lebanon while Hezbollah withstands a IDF operation to seize Bint Jbeil.

This event is highlighted because the ten day delay in Israel conducting a ground offensive is key. Hezbollah utilized the delay to fortify defensive sites, occupy southern Lebanese villages, lay obstacles and motivate the population to their cause. Hezbollah had very good tactical intelligence as they knew the likely routes of advance of Israeli forces. It also demonstrates that the historic Israeli response of an air war was not adequate in defeating Hezbollah.

5. 30 July 2006--Over 50 Lebanese civilians and more than thirty children killed in Qana, Lebanon by Israeli air strike, igniting international outrage. Israel announces a 48-hour cessation of air strikes, which it will later break, and 24-hours for Lebanese civilians to leave southern Lebanon through "humanitarian corridors" to be coordinated by the UN. UN says it was not given enough time to mobilize the effort. Hezbollah initiates a "payment program" to provide families compensation for their losses at the hands of Israel and offers medical assistance to communities.

This event demonstrates Hezbollah's significant IO capability. Despite the fact that Hezbollah was conducting a significant number of attacks against Israeli civilians, Hezbollah IO was successful in shaping world opinion and turning the world against

26

Israeli actions by highlighting their killing of Lebanese civilians. This partially goes to Hezbollah's presence in villages. Hezbollah fighters, many of whom are not even members of Hezbollah, occupied all southern villages. These fighters were trained and in position to quickly alert media of Israeli harm to civilians. In addition, this clearly demonstrates Hezbollah's actions to obtain legitimacy with the local population, the government of Lebanon and the world.

6. 4 August 2006--Israeli Prime Minister Ehud Olmert gives several interviews to the international press in which he affirms Israel's intention to cripple Hezbollah, but welcomes the role of an international peacekeeping force in the very near future and says Israel has no intention of broadening the fight to the rest of Lebanon. Meanwhile, Hezbollah leader Hassan Nasrallah warns Hezbollah will fire rockets at Tel Aviv if Israel attacks Beirut and an Iraqi Shia leader calls for a "million man march" in support of Hezbollah.

This key event demonstrates how Hezbollah was successful in keeping itself separate from the government of Lebanon reaffirming itself and actions as an independent organization conducting a "long war" or pro-longed insurgency against Israel. This also reaffirms Hezbollah's IO ability in that they put Israel on the defensive in the world press. The call for a "million man march" in Iraq demonstrates Hezbollah's reach and influence as well as network abilities and IO reach. The fact Hezbollah was threatening action to defend Beirut (i.e., Lebanon) demonstrates its advanced role in Lebanese government operations.

Evaluation Criteria

U.S. counterinsurgency doctrine will be compared against Hezbollah operations outlined previously using six evaluation criteria:

1. Decisive Concentration of Force--Make the best use of military power to destroy, expel or defeat the main body of armed insurgents.

This criteria includes effectively identifying all aspects of force available (lethal and nonlethal) and then identifying how to apply them in concert in order to achieve the commander's objectives. To effectively perform this criterion, doctrine must call for timely identification of assets that can affect a target, call for coordination between these assets, and concentration of these assets to defeat the main threat of the insurgency (does not have to directly target the main threat but must lead to its defeat).

2. Security--Measures taken to protect against all acts designed to, or which may, impair the effectiveness of the local government and security force.

In a COIN environment, security is often a perception that you must create in the eyes of the local population. The population will only trust a government that makes it feel safe and often COIN operations are a fight with an insurgency to obtain that legitimacy in the eyes of the population. To effectively perform this criterion, doctrine must recognize the need to secure the population, must recognize the significant role of indigenous forces as an agent of the local government and must emphasize the significance of maintaining security to achieve success.

3. Flexibility/adaptability--ability to respond to unexpected changes or actions and be able to modify one's plans/doctrine accordingly.

Because COIN operations are essentially a social struggle, defined by specific social, political and economic conditions of a nation, COIN is significantly dependent of flexibility. What works against one insurgency may not work against another due to the different circumstances. To be considered effective in terms of flexibility and adaptability, doctrine must be written in a manner that allows it to be applied to different problem sets while giving basic guidance on execution of operations. Doctrine should outline principles that apply to the defeat of any insurgency without causing complacency or pre-determining enemy's capabilities.

4. Objective--Every operation is directed toward a clearly defined, decisive and attainable objective (destruction of the enemy's ability to fight and will to fight).

In all operations the objective must be destruction of the enemy force but how you achieve that varies. Effective COIN doctrine will emphasize that every action conducted by a military force be with a clearly defined objective that will ultimately lead to the destruction of the insurgency. Doctrine must emphasize that every media report, every foot patrol and every bombing will affect the perception of military action (both your and the insurgency) in the eyes of the population, the enemy and the world.

5. Legitimacy--Excepted as the standard of law and governance; destroying the local insurgent political organizations and recognition as a governing/securing force.

Ultimately, COIN operations are derived to restore the legitimacy of a government while denying insurgents any claims of legitimacy. This legitimacy is derived from the population and therefore requires security and political, economic, and social development by the government. Legitimate governments engender the popular support required to manage internal problems, change, and conflict. Strategically speaking, it is as important for any COIN operation that the needs of the people are being met as the enemy is hunted down. Any sign of weakness of the government or lapse of security will be exploited and used by the insurgency to discredit the government. At the same time, U.S. forces cannot be seen as the lead entity in restoring security and social order in the eyes of the population. If the U.S. military, or any U.S. agency for that matter, undermines the legitimacy of the local government and sends the message that the government cannot provide these services on its own, lending credibility to the insurgency. Effective COIN doctrine will recognize that all actions must be directed at gaining credibility of the local government in the eyes of the population while simultaneously reducing the credibility of the opposing insurgency.

6. Sustainability – the ability to maintain operational capability/established standards.

There are two aspects to sustainability that must be met for doctrine to be considered effective in terms of this criterion. First, forces must be able to sustain the gains they have made during operations. This means that doctrine must adequately address assessment of forces needs, maintenance of security, and the ability to maintain gains in legitimacy. The second aspect is that the local government must be able to sustain established standards once U.S. forces withdraw. This means that local security forces must be trained and expanded as required and that local governments must accept their requirement to care for the population and provide basic services. In addition, local governments must have the capacity to provide this care and services which may mean training and expansion as well as funding.

Method of Evaluation

Chapter 4 will closely examine each of the six key events addressed previously. This examination will include an extensive look at how Hezbollah functioned and what unique abilities they demonstrated during each event. Following examination of an event, U.S. COIN doctrinal reactions will be examined. Using Israel's response to these key events will help in determining which grade (E = Effective, A=Adequate, I=Inadequate) U.S. doctrine will receive and an explanation for its success or failures will be provided. The following chapter will entail the conduct of this war game with results recorded on the following chart.

Table 1.   Evaluation Template

Event	1	2	3	4	5	6
Concentration of Force						
Security						
Flexibility						
Objective						
Legitimacy						
Sustainability						

CHAPTER 4

ANALYSIS

[T]he resistance withstood the attack and fought back. It did not wage a guerrilla war either…it was not a regular army but was not a guerrilla in the traditional sense either. It was something in between. This is the new model.

— Hasan Nasrallah
Hezbollah's Secretary General

Introduction

This paper will answer the primary question of whether US COIN doctrine is adequate to defeat Hezbollah as a threat model of future insurgencies. Key components of this are Hezbollah and their capabilities, lessons learned by Israel as Hezbollah's most frequent opponent, and U.S. COIN doctrine itself. In the 2006 Lebanon War, Israel was defeated by Hezbollah in most of the world's eyes. Considering Israel's history and frequent fights with insurgent groups trying to over through them and their existence, it came as a shock that Hezbollah was so successful against them. As a result, studying the failures of their doctrine as it applies to Hezbollah provides a strong foundation for reviewing our own doctrine and can serve as a basis for evaluating whether U.S. doctrine is adequate.

Methodology

To evaluate the effectiveness of U.S. COIN doctrine against Hezbollah, this paper will examine the six key events from the 2006 Lebanon War outlined in the previous chapter. Using these six events, this paper will examine Hezbollah's actions as representative of their capabilities and the likely threat model of future course of actions.

This will be followed by a critical description of Israeli response and then, using the six evaluation criteria laid out in the previous chapter, examine if U.S. COIN doctrine, as currently written, is adequate to defeat Hezbollah as a model of insurgent threat. The evaluation criteria were selected based on widely accepted ingredients critical to successful counterinsurgency operations and U.S. lessons learned in Iraq. Israel's response to Hezbollah's actions and Israeli lessons learned will be used to help judge whether U.S. response per COIN doctrine is adequate. U.S. COIN doctrine will be given an "E" to indicate that doctrine, as outlined, will be effective against Hezbollah as a threat model; an "A" for adequate-- meaning the response would have a positive effect though not a complete one; and an "I" for inadequate-- meaning that doctrine needs to be changed in order to effectively or even adequately address the threat.

War Game

12 July 2006

Event: Hezbollah launches rockets across the Lebanese border, targeting several Israeli border towns, and then stages an attack in which three Israeli soldiers are killed and two more kidnapped.

Key Issues: An insurgency initiates operations against civilian and military targets requiring an adequate response; one that protects civilian and military targets.

Hezbollah Initial Actions

This attack demonstrates the years of training and dedicated study of Israeli operations by Hezbollah. Hezbollah knew that Israel would rely heavily on air strikes and artillery precision weapons and limit its use of ground forces (Achcar 2007, 32). Based on this knowledge, Hezbollah conducted in-depth operational planning. Hezbollah formed several rocket teams and scattered rocket launchers in various villages. They established a simple, yet effective system for firing rockets which included multiple teams executing battle drills. One team would move into place the rockets, a second team moves into set up the launcher and a third team fires. The majority of rockets were fired from bunkers built underground to withstand precision air strikes (Erlanger 2006, 1,6). These positions had eighteen inches of concrete for overhead cover to provide protection from Israeli air strikes mitigating Israel's main weapon. Additional preparation included the acquisition of over 12,000 short-, medium-, and long-range ground to ground missiles from Iran and Syria. It is assessed that Iranian forces fielded and trained Hezbollah fighters on the use of these systems (Kulick 2007). Protecting firing units and locations included the fielding and utilization of anti-tank missiles, combined with expertly placed mines and IEDs along Israeli likely avenues of approach into southern Lebanon (Division IDF 91st 2009). While these preparations demonstrate Hezbollah's dedication to operational planning, their choosing to conduct the kidnapping of Israeli forces in the July months was a very strategic decision in that the mid-summer months greatly favor the static defender over a dismounted aggressor. Hezbollah obviously spent a considerable amount of time thinking about when to attack, how the IDF would fight, what weapons the IDF would use, as well as what personnel, fortifications and tactics they would need to apply. This also demonstrates Hezbollah's hybrid capability in that they utilize conventional weapon systems of a conventional army while employing guerilla warfare tactics.

Israeli Response

First, it is important to note that Israel, between 2000 and 2006 adopted doctrine based on the theories of precision fire power and Effects Based Operations (EBO). The Winograd Report attempted to explain the mind set of Israeli leaders when it pronounced, "Some of the political and military elites in Israel have reached the conclusion that Israel is beyond the era of wars. It had enough military might and superiority to deter others from declaring war against her; these would also be sufficient to send a painful reminder to anyone who seemed undeterred; since Israel did not intend to initiate war, the conclusion was that the main challenge facing the land forces would be low intensity asymmetrical conflicts. Given these assumptions, the IDF did not prepare for "real war." (Ha'aretz Staff 2007) As a result, Israel adopted EBO, the belief that they could destroy specific, targeted portions of its enemy with precision guided munitions, and achieve the desired effect of silencing the threat (Matthews 2008, 23). The combined result was an army that had not trained and was unprepared to respond to the threat posed by Hezbollah triggered by the kidnapping of Israeli soldiers. This lack of preparation was immediately evident as the Battalion Commander in charge of the kidnapped soldiers failed to adhere to standard operating procedure and move his forces into Lebanon to cut off Hezbollah routes to their safe havens. The commander feared mines and IEDs in the area and instead choose to wait for helicopters to arrive and conduct the search from air (Matthews, 35-36). Nearly two hours after the kidnapping, approximately three armored vehicles did enter southern Lebanon and were met by an IED followed by an engagement by Hezbollah ground forces. As a result, Israeli leaders began precision air strikes. What this clearly demonstrated to Hezbollah and the world was that the Israeli military had developed an over reliance on air and precision strikes and lost the ability to execute

basic ground operations. This included failure to disseminate basic intelligence, failure to

pass critical situation updates, and an unwillingness to execute ground operations.

U.S. COIN Doctrinal Response

Decisive Concentration of Force: Score--I. U.S. COIN doctrine is slightly

inconsistent in this area. Conducting combat operations in order to secure the

environment is a standing principle in U.S. doctrine, as is defining the problem and the

desired outcome. However, COIN doctrine does not place enough emphasis on defeating

threat elements through combat to sufficiently address the threat posed by Hezbollah

during this key event. Specifically, chapter 5 of FM 3-25, Executing Counterinsurgency

Operations, addresses the principles and tactics for executing COIN operations.

Paragraph 5-3 lays out the fact that COIN operations "combine offensive, defensive, and

stability operations to provide the stable and secure environment needed for effective

governance, essential services, and economic development" (U.S. Army 2006, 5-2). The

chapter goes on to explain that the initial stage of these operations can be viewed as "Stop

the Bleeding" and recognizes that the initial steps must be to protect the population, break

the insurgents' initiative and momentum, and set the conditions for further engagements.

This portion of doctrine sounds like the correct formula to defeat any insurgent threat

however, the chapter goes on to explain that "limited offensive operations may be

undertaken, but are complemented by stability operations focused on civil security." This

approach is similar to the approach taken by Israeli forces in that they engaged in limited

offensive operations, specifically standoff air operations, aimed at stopping the

immediate threat of Hezbollah forces. What Israel learned is that Hezbollah was not conducting "limited" operations and a robust ground force designed to defeat the threat in order to secure military forces would have been the first required step in these operations. Over all, it is determined that if the U.S. Army were to approach Hezbollah as an insurgency, and apply counter insurgency doctrine to address the immediate and initial actions of Hezbollah, our performance too would have been inadequate. Specifically, attempting to conduct simultaneous stability operations prior to eliminating what should be viewed as a conventional threat would have resulted in loss of life and delay of initial success.

Security: Score--A. FM 3-24 recognizes the significance of securing the environment as part of regaining the initiative. Specifically, paragraph 1-14 states that "before most COIN operations begin, insurgents have seized and exploited the initiative, to some degree at least. Therefore, counterinsurgents undertake offensive and defensive operations to regain the initiative and create a secure environment. . . . As counterinsurgents gain the initiative, offensive operations focus on eliminating the insurgent cadre, while defensive operations focus on protecting the populace and infrastructure from direct attack" (U.S. Army 2006, 1-3). This addresses Israel's initial failure to protect their own population and to take aggressive actions to eliminate Hezbollah. Despite this recognition, inadequate attention is given to obtaining security against a conventional threat as a means to conducting stability operations rather than a simultaneous act.

Flexibility/Adaptability: Score--A. Although U.S. doctrine as a whole allows for significant flexibility, COIN doctrine itself does not adequately allow for its application against an insurgency opposing what they view as occupying force (Hezbollah against

37

Israel) utilizing hybrid warfare. Counterinsurgency doctrine continuously addresses the importance of knowing the environment you are about to enter and understanding the objectives of the insurgent threat but does not apply well to a non-government entity protected by a state, attacking what it views as an occupying force, as is the case with Hezbollah. Paragraph 1-6 in FM 3-24 recognizes Hezbollah as an insurgency specifically stating that exceptions to normal patterns exist where "indigenous elements seek to expel or overthrow what they perceive to be a foreign or occupation government." (U.S. Army 2006, 1-6) Clearly Hezbollah views Israel as a government occupying territory that belongs to Lebanon and the Muslim world but doctrine does not adequately address how to approach such a threat when it is "protected" by a third party government. The basic principals outlined in U.S. COIN doctrine can be bent to allow for initial tactical success against a force that has initiated attacks against our forces but not operational or strategic success required for this complex dynamic.

Objective: Score--E. U.S. COIN doctrine clearly emphasizes the significance of campaign design and clearly defined objectives. Israel failed to determine exactly what they as a force were trying to achieve and most importantly failed to communicate these objectives to the force. Like all current U.S. Army doctrine, FM 3-24 emphasizes the importance of unity of effort and ensuring all lines of operation are focused on a well understood end state.

Legitimacy: Score--A. During the initial phases of COIN operations as depicted by this event, U.S. COIN doctrine emphasizes that legitimacy is obtained by securing the environment and includes the use of indigenous forces when possible. The role of legitimacy increases later in operations.

Sustainability: Score--A. This criterion is very difficult to measure with this key event. Considering the initial response U.S. COIN doctrine directs would be inadequate in defeating Hezbollah, it is difficult to judge adequate actions would be sustainable. Doctrine does repeatedly emphasize the point that COIN operations are long and protracted and that any actions must be sustainable.

14 July 2006

Event: Hezbollah fires rockets, causing major damage in the Israeli city of Haifa. Israel Prime Minister Ehud Olmert announces that in order for Israel to call a ceasefire, Hezbollah must disarm, end its rocket attacks on Israeli civilians, and return the kidnapped soldiers. Meanwhile, Syria pledges its full support of Hezbollah and Iranian president, Mahmoud Ahmadinejad, warns Israel not to attack Syria.

Key Issues: The insurgency is increasing the risk/danger toward the civilian population and threat of international support for the insurgency is becoming more pronounced.

Hezbollah Response

The significance of this day is not necessarily Hezbollah actions, but rather what they represent: the day the world began to understand the complex network of world supporters Hezbollah has. The massive support Iran and Syria have given Hezbollah since its founding increased significantly between 2000 and 2006 as both countries regard Lebanon as their "front line" against Israel (which they view as an "occupying force" on Arab soil) and Hezbollah as their strategic proxy (Byman 2008). This support essentially turned Hezbollah into an Iranian stronghold in the heart of the Arab world. The presence of a stronghold in Lebanon has given Iran cultural influence and political clout, increased its regional influence and enabled it to use terrorism against Israel without being directly linked. This has enabled the formation of an armed resistance movement, utilizing indigenous forces (Hezbollah), to expel what Iran and most Arab states view as an occupying government without any state having to risk state on state violence. This, in effect, provides Iran with a military option to both attack Israel and destabilize the region during a crisis. The Iranian Revolutionary Guards established Hezbollah and supported them by training their members, transmitting technical know-how, and providing weapons (through Damascus), ideological guidance and extremely generous funding (Harik 2005, 33-35). Between 2000 and 2006, Iran, with the help of Syria, focused on providing Hezbollah advanced military capability to augment guerilla operations. This includes providing them with rockets and constructing an arsenal of between 12,000 and 13,000 ground-to-ground missiles of various ranges. They also assisted by helping Hezbollah to formulate the operational plan utilizing Iranian military doctrine, which resulted in the kidnapping of two Israeli soldiers and the subsequent attacks and resistance. 14 July 2006 marked the realization that Iranian support for Hezbollah, through the Qods Force ("the Jerusalem [*Qods*] Force"), includes financing (more than $100 million annually), training in Iran and Lebanon, and supplying state-of-the arts weapons and intelligence about Israel. The Qods Force focused special attention on Hezbollah units operating weapons perceived as strategic, such as ground-to-ground rockets with a range of more than 75 kms (46 miles) and UAVs (Cordesman 2006, 22-25).

Israeli Response

Israeli response to the significant rocket attacks by Hezbollah and the support network it demonstrates will be viewed in three contexts: 1) the military response to rocket attacks, 2) the strategic significance of the rocket attacks, and 3) intelligence and non-military actions regarding the supply build up and Iranian support.

The military response to Hezbollah rockets attacks was restricted to a stand-alone air campaign. The objective of air strikes was not to directly target Hezbollah, forcing their destruction, but rather to produce effects that would force Hezbollah north of the Litani River and eventually force them to disarm (Ha'aretz Staff 2007). Specific targets of the attack included Hezbollah political and military leadership, symbolic Lebanese targets and military resources. The use of ground forces was dismissed as an option by top Israeli leadership early in the decision process and leaders recognized that the Lebanese government was not capable of putting any significant pressure on Hezbollah (Weitz 2006). Despite days of near constant rocket attacks, Israeli leaders failed to recognize that air strikes alone were not working and in fact only impacted seven percent of Hezbollah's military resources (Matthews 2008, 23-25). In addition, the IDF statement of its strategic goals presented to the Israeli government at the beginning of the conflict failed to even mention home-front defense leaving the security of the population as an afterthought or someone else's problem (Ha'aretz Staff 2007).

Israeli leaders failed to recognize the strategic significance of the large number of rockets in Hezbollah's arsenal. At the start of the 2006 conflict, the belief from previous wars still prevailed, the belief that rockets were weapons of little consequence because of their inaccuracy and small warheads. In the initial stage of the war, Israeli Secretary of

41

Defense Halutz said that "short range rockets are not a decisive weapon" (Ha'aretz Staff 2007). As a result of this attitude, the civilian population of Northern Israel was essentially left completely unprepared for the destruction these rockets brought. It is assessed that nearly 4,000 rockets/missiles launched hit urban areas and paralyzed the whole of northern Israel, its main port, refineries, and many other strategic installations (BBC Staff 2008). The continuous barrage of Katyushas Rockets on Israel's northern cities supported Hezbollah's claim to victory. Only in the last stages of the war did the attempt to limit the Katyusha's become an operational goal of Israel and there are no indications they addressed the strategic issues of where and how Hezbollah was able to build such an arsenal.

A large portion of these issues can likely be linked to Israeli intelligence and diplomatic failures. Over the course of several years, Israel's intelligence organizations had neglected to collect intelligence regarding Hezbollah's short range Katyushas rockets, there increased military capability, Hezbollah movements and actions and under reported Iran's massive support to Hezbollah. From the Israeli perspective, the Islamic regime in Iran presents a danger to its existence yet Israel does not appear to dedicate any of its vast intelligence networks to monitoring Iranian activities in its own back yard. The IDF intelligence had six years since the last war with Lebanon in which to collect information about the location and build up of Hezbollah rocket launchers, rocket depots, and the command and control centers of their enemy. The hundreds of rockets Hezbollah launched on a daily basis for four consecutive weeks indicate a colossal intelligence failure on the part of Israel. It is not clear whether the intelligence community warned the political leaders of the consequences of acting without detailed knowledge of the location of Hezbollah's rocket launchers and depots. Nor do we know whether the intelligence community provided the government with an accurate assessment of the military, political, and home front costs of a war. We do know that no government entity has provided the IDF guidance on what the desired out come for terrorist organizations attacking Israel is. To this day, the strategic objective of the Israeli government remains unknown to military leaders. A high ranking Israeli leader recently stated that "Either we want to achieve a sustainable arrangement, with a lasting cease-fire and a stop to arms smuggling from Egypt and Iran, or we want to bring about a collapse of the Hamas and Hezbollah governments," he said. "These lead to very different actions on all fronts, but the answer is not very clear. There is disagreement at the moment in the troika and as a result, the linkage between the political level and the military level is less improved." (Erlanger 2009) A source of the problem may be the fact that there is no political system in Israel for making strategic assessments. It is widely known that the center for strategic thinking in Israel is the military and as a result, diplomatic efforts and government direction are significantly lacking.

U.S. COIN Directed Response

Decisive Concentration of Force: Score--E. Decisive concentration of force at the point of this key event calls for using all instruments of national power to address the total threat being faced. This includes the external support Hezbollah received, intelligence directed at defining the extent of the threat, diplomacy toward Lebanon as well as the nations providing support to Hezbollah and a concentration of force against the tactical threat as well. The Winograd Report recognizes that Israel continued to limit actions to air strikes and very limited diplomatic actions directed at the UN and U.S.

while failing to expand military, diplomatic or intelligence efforts (Ha'aretz Staff 2009). U.S. COIN doctrine places significant emphasis on the fact that unity of effort among not only military forces but also civilian agencies and activities is critical to COIN success (U.S. Army 2006, 2-1 thru 2-14).

Security: Score--E. As Hezbollah increased its threat toward the civilian population of Israel, little to no effort was taken to secure the population of Israel against this threat; no action was taken to secure the Lebanese population against threat or danger and over emphasis was placed on preserving IDF life. As addressed in the previous key event, U.S. COIN doctrine does emphasize the significance of securing the population and if followed, U.S. forces would have placed far greater significance on all aspects of security then Israeli forces did. The main ingredient is scoring this criteria as effective, is that securing the population is addressed as paramount in U.S. COIN doctrine.

Flexibility/Adaptability: Score- I. U.S. COIN doctrine recognizes Hezbollah as an insurgency per FM 3-4, paragraph 1-6 and recognizes that non-state actors will be utilized by nation states as "proxies" to fight the U.S. indirectly, similar to how Iran and Syria is using Hezbollah to fight Israel. Despite these recognitions, U.S. COIN doctrine fails to provide guidance on how to approach a threat based in a bordering nation such as Israel has to face with Hezbollah in Lebanon or the U.S. with the Taliban in Pakistan. By the time forces reach this key event it is essential they be able to react to a broader threat than the traditional insurgency this doctrine was written to address (specifically local based threats).

Objective: Score--E. This key event defines the importance of having the right objective identified. In response to this threat, the objective should be securing the

44

population and stopping attacks for a pro-longed time. Instead, Israel continued to focus on creating a perception of defeat in the eyes of Hezbollah, failing to adjust their objective to the quick and total destruction of Hezbollah. U.S. COIN doctrine emphasizes, in chapter 4, paragraph 4-20 that "the mosaic nature of insurgencies and the shifting circumstances within each area of operation requires a different emphasis on and the interrelationship among the various lines of operation" (U.S. Army 2006, 4-5). The act of reassign areas of emphasis and reevaluating objectives and means is emphasized throughout FM 3-24 as necessary due to the fluidity of COIN operations. If following U.S. COIN doctrine, operations against Hezbollah would have been redirected against a new, more specific, clearly defined goal.

Legitimacy: Score--I. At the point of this key event, security and legitimacy are closely linked. U.S. COIN doctrine, in chapter 6, paragraph 6-6, addresses the significance of this linkage. Doctrine states that "A government reliant on foreign forces for internal security risks not being recognized as legitimate. While combat operations with significant U.S. and multinational participation may be necessary, U.S. combat operations are secondary to enabling the host nation's ability to provide for its own security" (U.S. Army 2006, 6-2). This passage raises more questions than it provides answers. As addressed previously, the situation with Hezbollah and Israel is not a traditional insurgent situation and is defined by FM 3-24 as "an exception to the pattern," but this passage fails to relay how to obtain security and legitimacy simultaneously and implies that legitimacy is more important, leading one to conclude that inaction, or limited action, is doctrinal.

Sustainability: Score--E. At the point of this key event, forces are still trying to obtain security, leaving little for doctrine to provide in terms of sustainability guidance. U.S. COIN doctrine does emphasize that separating an insurgency from its resources is the keys means of obtaining sustainable peace (U.S. Army 2006, 1-23). In this, doctrine advices cutting off sources that allow for an insurgency to recuperate and therefore allowing for sustain defeat of the insurgency. Had Israel placed emphasis on reducing supply and financial links to supporting nations, destroying rocket caches and targeting the right levels of Hezbollah networks as U.S. COIN doctrine advises, they may have had more success.

17 July 2006

Event: Israeli elite Special Forces known as the Maglan Unit, conducts limited battalion size ground operations into Hezbollah territory in Lebanon to find a network of tunnels and were quickly surrounded by Hezbollah fighters. The IDF was forced to commit three plus additional brigades to relieve the Maglan force as Hezbollah utilized antitank missiles to penetrate Israeli armor and defeat committed forces.

Key Issues: New intelligence reveals more sophisticated insurgency than originally assessed; insurgency gains tactical advantage by utilizing conventional weapons and tactics.

Hezbollah Response

The ability to surround Israel's most elite ground force demonstrates Hezbollah's tremendous tactical proficiency. Hezbollah utilized small arms, mortars, rockets, and antitank weapons in combined arms operations rather than the standard hit and run tactics commonly utilized by insurgent organizations. This shows that Hezbollah operates in cells that are task organized by mission and able to conduct simultaneous operations and demonstrates an ability of non-state actors to fight their own form of net-centric warfare. Essentially, Hezbollah acted as a "distributed network" of small cells and units acting with considerable independence, and capable of rapidly adapting to local conditions but able to come together to mass capabilities on one objective. Rather than have to react faster than the IDF's decision cycle, networked tunnels allowed Hezbollah to wait out Israeli attacks, staying in positions, re-infiltrating or reemerging from cover, and choosing the time to attack or ambush. Forward fighters could be left behind or sacrificed, and "self-attrition" became a tactic substituting for speed of maneuver and the ability to anticipated IDF movements. This combination of conventional and guerilla execution is likely a result of Iranian training. In effect, the Hezbollah formation in south Lebanon was the direct product of Iranian doctrine. Their military zone in south Lebanon was composed of a number of territorial brigades and anti-tank, artillery, logistics, engineering and communications units capable of massing these individual capabilities to achieve a desired effect as demonstrated by the surrounding and defeat of Israeli Maglan forces (Matthews 2008, 43-44). This is likely due to the fact that these units are subordinate to a kind of Hezbollah "general staff" located in the southern Beirut. In the 2006 war, the "general staff" had various functions such as a "strategic weapons" unit (ground-to-ground rockets) an aerial unit (UAVs), a marine unit and others (Erlanger 206, 1,6).

Israeli Response

Israel was all but forced to respond to Hezbollah surrounding its Maglan force with the commitment of additional ground forces, albeit, a temporary increase in ground

47

operations. Specifically, the IDF committed three additional armor brigades, elements of

the Golani Brigade, and engineer battalion and a paratrooper battalion. Prior to Hezbollah

success against the Maglan Forces, Secretary Halutz had no intention of committing more

than one brigade to ground operations. Hezbollah continued to experience success against

this increased number of forces as they utilized antitank missiles, small arms and mortars

with unanticipated expertise (Matthews 2008, 44). The Wagdon Report highlighted how

an inflated concern over casualties caused IDF commanders to become overly cautious in

operations. This report also confirmed that IDF forces and commanders were deficient in

basic tactical skills and the application of combined arms. It is assessed that years of

strictly executing COIN operations created a generation of officers and soldiers that were

inept at conventional operations (Ha'aretz Staff 2007).

U.S. COIN Directed Response

Decisive Concentration of Force: Score--E. In response to an increase in combat

operations and use of conventional weapons by Hezbollah, COIN doctrine encourages the

re-appropriation of operational emphasis. U.S. COIN doctrine recognizes three aspects to

counterinsurgency operations: stability, offense and defense. Doctrine states that all three

aspects must be applied simultaneously but commanders should adjust the weight given

to each area based on changes in the situation (U.S. Army 2006, 1-19). Using this

guidance, doctrine allows commanders to increase the emphasis on offensive operations

in order to relieve ambushed forces and defeat the threat.

Security: Score--A. Previous guidance regarding the significance of security, in

terms of both the population and force, remains unchanged regardless of change in events. Doctrine continues to require that actions taken help legitimize the host nation government and do nothing to transfer legitimacy to U.S. Forces.

Flexibility/Adaptability: Score--I. Israeli forces suffered from an over reliance on COIN doctrine and training and failed to give adequate attention to conventional combat operations. Although U.S. COIN doctrine recognizes the significance of offensive and defensive operations as elements of COIN, under emphasis continues in terms of applying conventional tactics against an insurgent threat under the circumstances that Israel faced.

Objective: Score--E. Israeli military leaders failed to adjust their objective toward defeating the force that successfully targets some of their most elite forces. As stated previously, U.S. COIN doctrine emphasizes the constant re-evaluation of objective, lines of operations and re-distribution of emphasis on the aspects of COIN. If followed, U.S. Commanders would have seen the directive in U.S. COIN doctrine to reassess and re-apply assets toward a new objective.

Legitimacy: Score--I. Although the issue of legitimacy is addressed over thirty times in FM 3-24, guidance fails to provide an effective way of promoting legitimacy in this circumstance. COIN doctrine addresses the significance of security, information operations, foreign internal defense, and many other aspects of COIN as essential in promoting the legitimacy of the host nation government. None of this guidance however helps commanders in determining how to deal with an insurgency of this nature and build legitimacy simultaneously. For Israel, building legitimacy means trying to get Hezbollah supporters to recognize their right to exist while promoting a "pro-Israel" Lebanese government. Building legitimacy of this nature does not fit into the limited guidance (sound bites) regarding legitimacy in FM 3-24.

Sustainability: Score--A. The same problem exists here as it did in the last key event. In order to sustain a solution, we must first reach one. Doctrine does provide guidance as to the importance of implementing lasting solutions and training host nation assets to maintain implemented solutions but it effectiveness cannot be adequately judged by this key event.

21 July 2006

Event: Israel initiated this key event by calling up its reservists, preparing for possible ground offensive in Lebanon while Hezbollah withstands an IDF operation to seize Bint Jbeil.

Key Issues: The insurgency holds key terrain deemed to give either side a strategic advantage; insurgency affectively resists friendly actions to seize the terrain by utilizing conventional weapons and techniques, denying friendly forces legitimacy in the eyes of population and world press.

Israeli Action

Israel initiated this key event by activating its reserve forces, and orders a Battalion to attack Bint Jbeil. The town of Bint Jbeil was very symbolic in this war effort. Hezbollah Secretary General Nasrallah delivered a victory speech from this location following Israeli troop withdrawals from Lebanon in 2000. Capturing this town would help Israel to achieve the perception of victory they sought under their new systemic operational design doctrine and hoped to create the perception of victory, forcing Hezbollah morale to drop and fighters to put down arms (IDF Division 2009).

Hezbollah Response

Hezbollah responded to Israeli actions by taking advantage of the delay created by activating reserve forces and utilized the ten day delay to fortify defensive sites, occupy southern Lebanese villages, laying obstacles and motivating the population to their cause. Hezbollah had very good tactical intelligence as they knew the likely routes of advance of Israeli forces into the area. This event also demonstrates that the historic Israeli response of an air war was not adequate in defeating Hezbollah but rather Hezbollah experienced enough success to force Israel to commit ground forces against the desire of the Secretary of Defense and forced them to call up their reserve forces. As Hezbollah forces met IDF advances with ambushes, Hezbollah's television station in al-Manar broadcast glowing reports of Hezbollah success (Matthews 2008, 46-47). These reports were relayed to Israeli viewers as well as an international audience.

U.S. COIN Directed Response

Decisive Concentration of Force: Score--E. Not only does U.S. COIN doctrine emphasize reallocating assets toward the most appropriate aspect of COIN operations, doctrine also emphasizes that COIN operations must be driven by intelligence. FM 3-24, Chapter 3, emphasizes that insurgents may use conventional means to conduct attacks as seen in this key event. It further dictates collection and assessment in order to drive commander's determination as to the appropriate level of response (U.S. Army 2006, 3-19). By emphasizing that intelligence drives COIN operations and that commander's use intelligence to determine the appropriate response, coupled with previous stated guidance on redistribution of combat power, applying U.S. COIN doctrine would have aided Israeli leaders in redirecting/concentrating efforts.

Security: Score--A. This key event does not call for a doctrinal change to security operations. Emphasis continues to be placed on securing the force and population. Israeli response was similar to a U.S. doctrinal response in that they surged forces to secure elements on the objective. U.S. doctrine also calls for additional efforts to be made to secure the population in the area and ensure their needs are being met.

Flexibility/Adaptability: Score--A. This specific key event does not challenge the flexibility/adaptability of U.S. COIN doctrine.

Objective: Score--E. The call by U.S. COIN doctrine to constantly re-evaluate objectives, lines of operation and re-distribute assets to place emphasis on the aspects of COIN ensures that despite changes brought on b this key event, responses will continue to focus on a unified objective.

Legitimacy: Score--I. The aspects of promoting legitimacy outlined in FM 3-24 are not applicable to this key event. COIN doctrine emphasizes using local security forces, interacting with local leaders and promoting the host nation government through IO. Emphasizing legitimacy through these actions is suppose to be done simultaneous to any U.S. combat operations but may not be possible in terms of this specific event.

Sustainability: Score--I. U.S. COIN doctrine emphasizes targeting aspects of an insurgency that can lead to their long term destruction as a means of sustaining security and stability in the area. In addition, training local security forces to address insurgent threats, and promoting an effective government are viewed as actions that can be taken to ensure success is sustainable. This key event does not call of any of these as an effective means dealing with legitimacy at this phase of operations.

30 July 2006

Event: Over 50 Lebanese civilians and more than thirty children are killed in Qana, Lebanon by an Israeli air strike, igniting international outrage. Israel announces a 48-hour cessation of air strikes, which it will later break, and 24-hours for Lebanese civilians to leave southern Lebanon through "humanitarian corridors" to be coordinated by the UN. The UN says it was not given enough time to mobilize the effort. Hezbollah initiates a "payment program" to provide families compensation for their losses at the hands of Israel and offers medical assistance to communities.

Key Issues: Insurgency conducts highly effective IO operations and begins significant actions to gain legitimacy in the eyes of the population.

Hezbollah Response

This event demonstrates Hezbollah's significant IO capability. Despite the fact that Hezbollah indiscriminately fired on Israeli civilians, they were able to utilize their robust IO network to highlight Israeli strikes on Lebanese citizens and successfully paint Israel as an army that disregards civilian life. This demonstrates a rather unique and significant capability Hezbollah possesses among threat organizations. As a non-state actor, it is not a surprise when they act in disregard for international rule of law but a skilled IO ability allows them to highlight an opponent's violation of these laws to the world. In addition, Hezbollah's success at IO can be credited to their presence among the population. Hezbollah fighters, many of whom are not even members of Hezbollah, occupied all southern villages. These fighters were trained and in position to quickly alert media of Israeli harm to civilians. In addition, this clearly demonstrates Hezbollah's actions to obtain legitimacy with the local population, the government of Lebanon and the world. Quick actions by Hezbollah to provide for the population and compensate for Israeli damage, is central to their ability to win the "hearts and minds" of not only the people of Lebanon, but worldwide public opinion.

Israeli Response

It appeared to most observers that Israel choose to simply ignore the bad press and IO success of Hezbollah and continue on with small battalion and brigade size raids into southern Lebanon. The Jewish Institute for National Security Affairs reports that senior members of the IDF advised an aggressive ground campaign aimed at eliminating Katyusha Rocket attacks. These leaders reported advised that if the Government did not permit a large scale ground offensive, the government should stop the campaign (Matthews 2008, 58). The fact that Israel failed to increase ground operations, ignored the success Hezbollah was having in the media and the legitimacy they were building in the eyes of the people of Lebanon and the world community, shows a significant lack of flexibility on the part of Israeli leaders and a lack of a strategic objective.

U.S. COIN Directed Response

Decisive Concentration of Force: Score--E. U.S. COIN doctrine emphasizes the application of IO by all levels of command and all forces, civilian and military, engaged in operations. Appendix A to FM 3-24 emphasizes the "global reach of today's news media affects the conduct of military operations more than ever before. . . . Train soldiers and Marines to consider how the global audience might perceive their actions" (U.S. Army 2006, A-5 thru A-6). By emphasizing that information operations' stem from all aspects of operations and all echelons, U.S. COIN doctrine focuses a concentrated effort on countering insurgent reports. In addition, U.S. COIN doctrine takes a similar approach to addressing the needs of the population. It emphasizes that COIN operations can be viewed as "armed social work". Doctrine points out that in executing civil-military operations, there must be close cooperation between national, international and local interagency and inter service partners. These are two examples of how COIN doctrine helps to ensure that all forces are concentrated on the outcome.

Security: Score--E. U.S. Coin doctrine emphasizes the importance of securing the local population and conducting operations in a manner that limits collateral and unnecessary damage. Chapter one of FM 3-24 emphasizes that "Any use of force produces many effects, not all of which can be foreseen. The more force applied, the greater the chance of collateral damage and determent to the security environment" (U.S. Army 2006, 1-27). By placing emphasize on controlling force and limiting collateral damage, COIN doctrine may have adequately prevented U.S. forces from entering the same complicated position IDF forces found themselves in.

Flexibility/Adaptability: Score--E. This key event marks two strong areas of U.S. COIN doctrine – securing the population and IO. As a result, this event does not test the flexibility/adaptability of the doctrine well. Doctrine does continuously emphasize the importance of being first to report the truth, helping commanders to provide appropriate response regardless of the circumstance.

Objective: Score--E. Repeated themes throughout FM 3-24 include concentrating all operations on protecting/securing the population and ensuring that all efforts stand up to global media scrutiny. By continually emphasizing the importance of these factors, U.S. COIN doctrine focuses all elements of COIN operations on ensuring the objectives of IO and security are achieved.

Legitimacy: Score--E. Israel lost significant legitimacy in the eyes of the world for not minimizing collateral damage while conducting air operations. Failure of Israel to conduct effective IO and counter Hezbollah IO operations further hurt their legitimacy while raising the legitimacy of Hezbollah. By calling for forces to minimize collateral damage, reimburse locals for military damage U.S. forces do cause , and promoting open dialogue with the media, U.S. COIN guidance provides solid guidance to help U.S. forces gain/maintain legitimacy during this key event.

Sustainability: Score--E. The standards of minimizing collateral damage and open dialogue are things easy to teach/train host nation forces to sustain. These actions can become part of tactics, techniques and procedures with minimal effort therefore sustainment is easily achieved.

4 August 2006

Event: Israeli Prime Minister Ehud Olmert gives several interviews to the international press in which he affirms Israel's intention to cripple Hezbollah, but welcomes the role of an international peacekeeping force in the very near future and says Israel has no intention of broadening the fight to the rest of Lebanon. Meanwhile, Hezbollah leader Hassan Nasrallah warns Hezbollah will fire rockets at Tel Aviv if Israel attacks Beirut and an Iraqi Shia leader calls for a "million man march" in support of Hezbollah.

Key Issues: The insurgency is broadening its political legitimacy by protecting its supporting government entities; the insurgency continues to receive international support while the UN works toward establishment of a cease fire.

Hezbollah Response

This event demonstrates how Hezbollah was successful in keeping itself separate from the government of Lebanon reaffirming itself and actions as an independent organization conducting a "long war" or pro-longed insurgency against Israel. The fact Hezbollah was threatening action to defend Beirut (i.e., Lebanon) demonstrates its advanced role in Lebanese government operations. This also reaffirms Hezbollah's IO ability in that they put Israel on the defensive in the world press. The fact that Hezbollah allowed the 10,000 soldier IDF to advance no more than four miles into southern Lebanon is perhaps the greatest example of their tactical proficiency. Hezbollah quickly became heroes among the Islamic world. The call for a "million man march" in Iraq demonstrates Hezbollah's reach and influence as well as network abilities and IO reach.

Israeli Response

Israel followed the announcement that the UNSC unanimously approved Resolution 1701, calling for a cease-fire and the end of the war, with an expansion effort. Knowing the war would soon end, Israeli defense leaders ordered multiple Division's to advance to the Litani River in an attempt to cease ground and put Israel in a position of power during cease-fire talks. After action reports revealed that commanders did not understand their orders or why the directive to continue north was given. As a result, units failed to synchronize operations and many failed to achieve their mission.

U.S. COIN Directed Response

Decisive Concentration of Force: Score--E. Decisive concentration of force at the time of this key event calls for using all instruments of national power to address the international support to Hezbollah. This includes focusing all elements of national power

57

together intelligence on international support networks, diplomacy toward Lebanon as an effort to enhance their ability to defeat Hezbollah, as well as concentration of force against the tactical threat. U.S. COIN doctrine places significant emphasis on the fact that unity of effort among not only military forces but also civilian agencies and activities is critical to COIN success (U.S. Army 2006, 2-1 thru 2-14).

Security: Score--E. U.S. COIN doctrine recognizes the importance of maintaining an adequate presence until security operations can be passed on to a trained and qualified force. In chapter 5, FM 3-24 highlights this as the final stage in COIN operations and states that "at this stage, the host nation has established or reestablished the systems needed to provide effective and stable government that sustains the rule of law. The government secures its citizens continuously, sustains and builds legitimacy through effective governance" (U.S. Army 2006, 5-2). It is understood that these functions may be handed over to another, competent and qualified force to perform these continued functions.

Flexibility/Adaptability: Score--A. Consistent with U.S. Army culture, FM 3-24 cannot be applied to failing operation as it does not provide adequate guidance on how to end operations if host nation forces are not capable of assuming security and governance and no additional party comes in to relieve U.S. operations. At the point of this key event, Israel has been unable to secure its own population, eliminate the threat, or win the support of the Lebanese population or government. As a result, our doctrine would not have been an adequate substitute as a means of guidance in concluding operations in Lebanon. The fact that U.S. COIN doctrine cannot be adapted to apply to this key event limits its flexibility/adaptability.

Objective: Score--E. U.S. COIN doctrine clearly emphasizes the significance of campaign design and clearly defined objectives. Israel failed to determine exactly what they as a force were trying to achieve and most importantly failed to communicate these objectives to the force. Like all current U.S. Army doctrine, FM 3-24 emphasizes the importance of unity of effort and ensuring all lines of operation are focused on a well understood end state.

Legitimacy: Score--E. U.S. COIN doctrine clearly emphasizes handing off responsibilities to a trained and qualified host nation security force and government (U.S. Army 2006, 6-1 thru 6-22). All efforts are directed at increasing the legitimacy of the host nation government and ensuring the population accepts them as a governing entity.

Sustainability: Score--A. U.S. COIN doctrine calls for peace and stability to be sustained by host nation or a third party security force. Since security and stability have not been obtained, and Hezbollah continues to achieve IO superiority, sustaining operations is not applicable.

Evaluation

Table 2.   Completed Evaluation

Event	1	2	3	4	5	6
Concentration of Force	I	E	E	E	E	E
Security	A	E	A	A	E	E
Flexibility	A	I	I	A	E	A
Objective	E	E	E	E	E	E
Legitimacy	E	I	I	I	E	E
Sustainability	A	E	A	I	E	E

Examination of Evaluation/Conclusion

This war game concludes that U.S. COIN doctrine is not adequate in itself to

address Hezbollah as the threat model for future insurgencies. Overall, this war game

determined that current doctrine does not address the operational and strategic level

challenges encountered by Israel in the key events examined here. At the operational and

strategic level, doctrine must address the emerging threat of insurgent elements taking

advantage of struggling governments to utilize ungoverned territory, referred to here after

as contested zones, to plan and prepare for operations against a target government in a bordering state. Israel experienced this as Hezbollah utilized Lebanon for basing and staging operations against Israel who they viewed as an occupying force. The U.S. is currently experiencing a similar challenge in confronting Taliban forces utilizing neighboring Pakistan for attacks against U.S. forces. At the tactical level, the war game was conclusive in determining that U.S. counterinsurgency doctrine is effective against Hezbollah where they mirror or operated similar to the common tactics and procedures used by insurgent organizations (guerilla and terrorist tactics). In areas where Hezbollah utilized conventional military tactics and more advanced irregular warfare tactics, U.S. COIN doctrine proved less effective. The following will exam the key findings in terms of criteria and key events.

U.S. COIN doctrine proved effective in the areas of Decisive Concentration of Force and Objective. The likely reason for U.S. COIN doctrinal success in these areas is that they are not changed by threat actions or TTP's. Unlike these two criteria, the four remaining criteria of security, flexibility/adaptability, legitimacy and sustainability are all highly affected by enemy actions. As a result, this paper determines that the areas affected by enemy action require additional doctrine to adequately support operations.

Specifically, the four remaining areas (security, flexibility/adaptability, legitimacy and sustainability) were negatively affected by the escalation of enemy activity to include the use of conventional tactics and weapons. The greatest factor in this area was how to simultaneously conduct stability operations while security remains threatened by major combat operations. This cannot rely on the application of operational doctrine alone as Hezbollah is more than a military force, and therein lays its real strength. It has political, social, diplomatic, and informational components that provide bedrock support for its military organization. That foundation, established by years of providing humanitarian aid, building physical infrastructure, educating Lebanese, and serving as medical providers would remain even in the aftermath of military defeat. Doctrine that better addresses how to simultaneously apply conventional and non-conventional military capabilities in support of integrated government operations is required.

The nature of the key events also had significant impact on war games results. Events five and six are where U.S. COIN doctrine proved most effective. The key issues of these events being: 1. Insurgency conducts highly effective IO operations and begins significant actions to gain legitimacy in the eyes of the population; 2. Insurgency is broadening its political legitimacy by protecting supporting government entities; the insurgency continues to receive international support while the UN works toward establishment of a cease fire. Of all six key events war gamed, these events most closely fall in lines with anticipated activities of standard insurgent operations. Both events focus on the insurgent organization conducting effective IO operations to win the support of the local populace. Current U.S. COIN doctrine specifies that the core of COIN operations is the struggle for the population's support (U.S. Army 2006, 1-28). As a result, it can be expected that COIN doctrine would perform well against these traditional key events.

In areas where Hezbollah utilized escalating hybrid tactics, COIN doctrine did not prove effective. U.S. COIN doctrine proved ineffective in areas where forces face simultaneous conventional weapons and tactics while trying to secure the population and build host nation legitimacy. U.S. COIN guidance focuses on guerilla style hit and run tactics versus prolonged engagements from a conventional force. To make the situation more complicated, Hezbollah operated from within Lebanon, utilizing Lebanon as a safe haven. Lebanon itself is either unwilling to or incapable of addressing Hezbollah. This situation could be considered isolated and not worthy of doctrinal attention however we are facing a very similar situation in Afghanistan. The Taliban is able to escape to relative safety in Pakistan where the government is incapable of providing adequate assistance to U.S. forces. The U.S. Army requires doctrine that provides guidance at the operational and strategic level to target an insurgency that operates in a third party country and utilizes hybrid tactics in an effort to overthrow an existing government. The development of an Irregular Warfare Doctrine that highlights hybrid warfare, as conducted by Hezbollah, as a likely future contingency operation, with current U.S. COIN doctrine as one subset, would meet the requirement. The following chapter will summarize and provide more specific recommendations to enhance doctrine.

CHAPTER 5

CONCLUSION

The state on state conflicts of the 20th century are being replaced by Hybrid Wars and asymmetric contests in which there is no clear-cut distinction between soldiers and civilians and between organized violence, terror, crime and war.

— Alan Dupont
Director, International Security Studies at the University of Sydney

Introduction

This paper answers the primary question of whether US COIN doctrine is adequate to defeat Hezbollah as a threat model of future insurgencies. Key components in determining that COIN doctrine is not adequate to defeat Hezbollah are Hezbollah and their capabilities, lessons learned by Israel as Hezbollah's most frequent opponent, and U.S. COIN doctrine itself. In the 2006 Lebanon War, Israel was defeated by Hezbollah in most of the world's eyes. Considering Israel's history and frequent fights with insurgent groups trying to over through them and their existence, it came as a shock that Hezbollah was so successful against them. As a result, studying their failures as they apply to Hezbollah provides a strong foundation for reviewing our own doctrine and can serve as a basis for evaluating whether U.S. doctrine is adequate. To conduct this evaluation, this paper examined six key events from the 2006 Lebanon War as outlined in chapter 3. Using these six events, this paper examined Hezbollah's actions as representative of their capabilities and the likely threat model of future course of actions followed by a critical description of Israeli response and then, using six evaluation criteria selected based on widely accepted ingredients critical to successful counterinsurgency operations, this paper examined if U.S. COIN doctrine, as currently written, is adequate to defeat Hezbollah as a model of insurgent threat.

Findings

This paper concludes that current COIN doctrine does not adequately address Hezbollah as a threat model and that the U.S. Army needs to dedicate time and expertise to studying operations against an insurgency utilizing hybrid tactics to further develop doctrine. Current doctrine is inadequate to address the complex, simultaneous blending of conventional and irregular tactics in the struggle to achieve political objectives. The 2006 Lebanon War demonstrates how, by mixing an organized political movement with decentralized cells employing adaptive irregular and conventional tactics in ungoverned zones, Hezbollah was able to inflict significant tactical, operational and strategic level damage against a modern conventional force. The war game conducted in this paper highlights and that current U.S. doctrine is not adequate to provide an established procedure for addressing what is likely to become a familiar operation.

This paper found that the first area currently lacking adequate analysis and doctrinal guidance is the operational and strategic level challenges of facing a hybrid threat, especially when operating from a third country sanctuary and/or with nation state support. Hezbollah has clearly demonstrated, through operations against Israel, that receiving support in the form of training, supplies and funding, from nation states provides such threat organizations with capabilities previously seen only in conventional armies. The situation becomes more complicated when a third party nation, either willingly or unwillingly, provides security through shared borders with the targeted nation as seen with Israel and Lebanon or with Afghanistan and Pakistan. It is assessed that future threat elements will continue to take advantage of ungoverned or poorly governed territory like these in order to offset conventional superiority of opponents. Frank G. Hoffman, in "The Rise of Hybrid Wars" refers to these as contested zones. He states that "The hybrid challenger realizes that complex terrain affords defenders a number of advantages that offset our conventional superiority. Recent combat operations suggest a shift towards what can be called contested zones. These zones include ungoverned ground, the dense urban jungles and the congested littorals where the majority of the world's population and economic activity is centered. Engaging American forces in the "contested zone" with a range of crude yet effective asymmetric approaches is intended to draw out conflicts, protract their duration and costs, and sap American will" (Hoffman 2007, 15). Hezbollah and the Taliban represent a growing threat where insurgent organizations undermine the will of existing weak states, to de-legitimize it, and stimulate a security break down, allowing them as non-state actors, to have freedom of movement. This provides these threat elements unprecedented security and sanctuary for planning, resourcing and mobilizing their efforts against a third party force such as Israel or the United States. Current literature and doctrine for defeating an insurgency does not address the significance of ungoverned territories and third party nations nor does it provide commanders with adequate guidance or procedures for addressing a threat utilizing these capabilities.

The second area not adequately covered by current COIN doctrine is how to successfully address the complexity, fusion, and simultaneity hybrid conflicts present at the operational and tactical levels where the enemy is fusing a full range of methods and modes of conflict simultaneously on one battle field. Current COIN doctrine proved effective in this war game at combating Hezbollah where they applied the traditional approaches utilized by insurgent organizations. Additionally, U.S. operational doctrine has proven effective at defeating a conventional force utilizing conventional combat operations. However, neither of these pieces of Army doctrine provides the means or the innovative thinking, experimentation, nor constant adaption that is required in our armed forces to defeat a hybrid threat simultaneously conducting both forms of warfare. Shortfalls were identified in the areas of securing a local population when the threat is engaging with the purpose of becoming operationally decisive, thereby extending the cost of security, rather than just protracting the conflict. This becomes an even greater issue when this is being conducted in densely populated urban areas. To further complicate the issue, security of the population and legitimacy of the host nation government are intertwined. How does a force bring legitimacy to a government in an area where they cannot secure the population or prevent massive loss of life? Current doctrine recognizes that these principles are intertwined but does not address how to achieve these complicated goals against a decisive threat.

Recommendations

The primary recommendation resulting from this paper is that the U.S. Army studies the concept of hybrid warfare and exam how to devise doctrine and forces to meet these inevitable threats. The organization or agency studying this emerging threat should begin by familiarizing themselves with the 2006 Lebanon War and Hezbollah tactics, techniques and procedures utilized in the conflict. This body needs to consider developing and adopting an irregular warfare doctrine that looks at COIN as just one subset of irregular warfare, focusing instead on an enemy that uses the threat of violence for influence over populations through a full range of military and other capabilities aimed at reducing their adversaries power, influence, and will. This doctrine needs to be centered on the fact that the Army of the future must refrain from thinking of war and military operations in linear formations and conventional conflicts as we must be as asymmetrical and adaptive as the threat.

Any change in military doctrine and structure must recognize that there are only so many training hours in a day, and only so many soldiers in the Army. Any time devoted to training on one form of war and military operations is time away from the other. Units cannot excel at everything simultaneously. The decision to concentrate effort and training on any one specialty over another requires a sound understanding of all options and future threats. Hybrid warfare, as demonstrated by Hezbollah, makes clear that there is no risk free option in concentrating U.S. efforts. The positive is that investing in the creation of adequate and complete doctrine is a minimal investment that can pay high dividends.

At the tactical level, doctrine should address the fact that irregular warfare, to include hybrid war, is very difficult and at the company and platoon level is intrinsically harder than conventional war fighting. In conventional operations, both friendly and enemy forces move in accordance with synchronized plans, executing doctrinal events that are relatively simple on the individual level. In hybrid war, as in irregular war, tactical units must be very agile and highly capable at multiple tasks which they must perform for extended periods of time. Though this challenge exists in COIN operations, it is compounded by hybrid war where enemy forces are now fighting to maintain terrain rather than conducting hit and run type guerilla tactics, and employing conventional

68

weapon technology to advance their goals. This requires a balance between conventional combat capability and COIN capabilities. This new balance should combine the conventional war fighting capability the army mastered prior to 2003 but also prepare soldiers for more protracted and complex missions of stability and nation building.

Any solution should look at placing operational emphasis at the company and platoon level and examine creating imbedded Special Forces like teams. These teams should be robust and integrated combined arms teams, capable of adapting their mode of operations and tailoring their forces against irregular and hybrid enemies as needed. Forces at the tactical level must possess highly trained skills at close quarter battle with the ability to close with and defeat opponents who are highly skilled in blending into their environment. This force must then be able to quickly transition to protecting and controlling a large number of local people in densely populated areas which likely contains the same fighters they were earlier engaged with. These organizations must contain organic intelligence assets robust enough to conduct predictive analysis and anticipate a highly adaptive enemy.

Because of the success Hezbollah experienced in 2006, we know that the application of hybrid tactics by threat forces will increase. Insurgencies have demonstrated that they are truly learning organizations. These threat elements study one another and adopt successful tactics, techniques and procedures as well as studying conventional armies to adopt conventional skills and capabilities while determining how to defeat us. This paper seeks to accelerate our own learning and hopes to influence leaders to become as adaptive and transforming as our enemy.

BIBLIOGRAPHY

Achcar, Gilbert. *The 33 day war, Israel's war on Hezbollah.* Boulder, CO: Paradigm Publishers, 2007.

U.S. Army. Field Manual (FM) 3-24, *Counterinsurgency.* Washington, DC: Government Printing Office, 2006.

Bacevich, Andrew. *The Limits of Power: The end of American exceptionalisions.* New York: Metropolitan Books, 2008.

BBC. "Timeline: Lebanon." *BBC World News,* 15 August 2008. http://news.bbc.co.uk/ 2/hi/middle_east/country_profiles/819200.stm (accessed 8 September 2008).

Biddle, Stephen and Jeffrey Friedman. *The 200 Lebanon Campaign and the Future of Warfare: Implications for Army and Defense Policy.* Washington, DC: Strategic Studies Institute, 2008.

Brynjar, Lia. *Globalization and the Future of Terrorism.* New York: Routledge, 2006.

Byman, Daniel L. "Hezbollah: Most Powerful Political Movement in Lebanon." *Counsel on Foreign Relations.* 29 May 2008. http://www.cfr.org/publication/16378/ powerful_movement.html?breadcrumb=%2F (accessed 2 October 2008).

Byman, Daniel. *Understanding Proto-Insurgencies.* Santa Monica, CA: RAND Corporation, 2007.

Cobban, Helena. "Hezbollah's New Face." *Boston Review,* April 2005. http://bostonreview.net/ BR30.2/cobban.html (accessed 22 September 2008).

Cordesman, Anthony H. "Preliminary Lessons of the Israeli-Hezbollah War." *Center for Strategic and International Studies*, 2006.

Court, Anderson. *Assessing the Aftermath: The Middle East After the Israeli-Hezbollah War.* Washington, DC: The Brookings Institution, 2006.

Crane, Conrad C. "Minting COIN, Principles and Imperatives for Combating Insurgency." *Air and Space Power Journal,* December 2007.

Division, IDF 91st. *Galilee Division Briefing.* Unit Presentation, Israeli IDF, 2009.

Erlanger, Steven and Richard Opper. "A Disciplined Hezbollah Surprises Israel With its Training, Tactics and Weapons." *New York Times*, 7 August 2006.

Erlanger, Steven. "For Israel, 2006 Lessons but Old Pitfalls." *New York Times,* 6 January 2009. http://www.nytimes.com/2009/01/07/world/middleeast/ 07military.html (accessed 22 February 2009).

Erlich, Reuven. "Hezbollah's use of Lebanese Civilians as Human Shields." *Intelligence and Terrorism Information Center,* 8 September 2006. http://www.terrorism-info.org.il/malam_multimedia/English/eng_n/ html/iran_hezbollah_e1b.htm (accessed 30 March 2009).

Glenn, Russell W. "Metamorphosis in Conflict." Proceedings of the Israeli Armored Corps Association "Winning Land Warfare After the Second Lebanon War" Conference. Tel Aviv: RAND Corporation, 2008.

Gomport, David C. and John Gordon. "War by Other Means." *RAND Counterinsurgency Study.* Santa Monica : RAND Corporation, 2008.

Gurney, David H. and Jeffrey D. Smotherman. "An Interview with George W. Casey Jr." *Joint Forces Quarterly* (1st quarter 2009).

Ha'aretz Staff. "The Winograd Report*." Ha'aretz.com,* 3 June 2007. http://www.ha'aretz.com/hasen/spages/854051.html (accessed 11 January 2009).

Harik, Judith Palmer. *Hezbollah, The Changing Face of Terrorism.* London: I.B. Tauris, 2005.

Hoffman, Frank G. "Conflict in the 21st Century: The Rise of Hybrid Wars." *Potomac Institute for Policy Study*, 2007.

Hoffman, Frank. "Lessons From Lebanon: Hezbollah and Hybrid Wars." *Foreign Policy Research Institue*, August 2006.

Jorisch, Avi. "Al-Manar and the War in Iraq." *Middle East Intelligence Bulletin,* April 2003. http://www.meib.org/articles/0304_11.htm (accessed 13 September 2008).

Kozayrn, Linda D. "American Forces Press Service News Articles." *Defenselink.mil.* 24 May 2002. http://www.defenselink.mil/news/newsarticle.aspx?id=44019 (accessed 1 October 2008).

Kreps, Sarah E. "The 2006 LebanonWar." *Parameters* (Spring 2007).

Kulick, Amir. "The Next War with Hizbollah." *Institute for National Security Studies.* December 2007. http://www.inss.org.il/ publications.php?cat=21&incat=&read=1383 (accessed 26 December 2007).

Mandari, Blanca. "Hezbollah's Global Finance Network: The Triple Frontier*." Middle East Intelligence Bulletin.* January 2002. http://www.meib.org/articles/ 0201_12.htm (accessed 4 October 2008).

71

Marrero, Abe F. "Hezbollah as a Non-State Actor in the Second Lebanon War: An Operational Analysis." Fort Leavenworth, KS: TRADOC/CSI Military History Conference, 2007.

Matthews, Matt M. *We Were Caught Unprepared: The 2006 Hezbollah-Israeli War,* OP 26, Fort Leavenworth: U.S. Army Combined Arms Center, 2008.

Myre, Greg and Steven Erlanger. "Clashes spread to Lebanon as Hezbollah raids Israel." *The International Herald Tribune* (12 September 2006). http://www.iht.com/articles/2006/07/13/africa/web.0712mideast.php (accessed 8 October 2008).

Ninan, Reena. "Chertoff: Hezbollah Makes Al Qaeda Look 'Minor League'." *Fox News,* 29 May 2008. http://www.foxnews.com/story/0,2933,359594,00.html (accessed 12 September 2008).

Norton, Augustus R. *Hezbollah, A short History.* Princeton, NJ: Princeton University Press, 2007.

Ophir, Noam. *Back to Ground Rules: Some Limitations of Airpower and Intelligence in the Lebanon War.* Strategic Assessment, Tel Aviv: Jaffee Center for Strategic Studies, 2006.

Qassem, Naim. *Hizbullah, The Story from Within.* London, ENG: Saqi, 2005.

Rao, Parshant. "Analysis: Hezbollah a force to be reckoned with." *The International Institute for Strategic Studies.* 18 July 2006. http://www.iiss.org/whats-new/iiss-in-the-press/press-coverage-2006/july-2006/hezbollah-a-force-to-be-reckoned-with/ (accessed 24 September 2008).

Staff, CFR.org. "Hezbollah (a.k.a. Hizbollah, Hizbu'llah)." *Counsel on Foreign Relations,* 13 August 2008. http://www.cfr.org/publication/9155/#6 (accessed 22 September 2008).

Telhami, Shibley. "Lebanese Identity and Israeli Security in the Shadows of the 2006 War." Blues.indd, 2006.

Thomas, Timothy L. "Hezballah, Israel, and Cyber PSYOP." *IO Sphere* (Winter 2007).

Trinquer, Roger. *Modern Warfare: A French View of Counterinsurgency,* Paris: Praeger International, 1961.

Unknown. *The Hezbollah Program, Stand By Us,* 29 October 2007. http://www.standwithus.com.asp (accessed 11 September 2008).

US State Department. "Background Information on Foreign Terrorist Organizations." Center for *Coordination for Counter Terrorism.* 30 April 2001.

http://www.state.gov/s/ct/rls/pgtrpt/2000/index.cfm?docid=2437 (accessed 22 September 2008).

Weitz, Paul. "Hezbollah, Already a Capable Military Force, Makes Full Use of Civilian Shields and Media Manipulation." *The Jewish Institute for Security Affairs,* 12 August 2006. http://www.jinsa.org/articles/articles.html/function/view/categoryid/158/documentid/3504/history/3,2360,655,158,3504 (accessed 11 October 2008).

www.ingramcontent.com/pod-product-compliance
Lightning Source LLC
Chambersburg PA
CBHW081848280526
45789CB00007B/2611